It's Friday,-
but
Sunday's
Comin'

Other books by Anthony Campolo

A Reasonable Faith: Responding to Secularism
A Denomination Looks at Itself
The Success Fantasy
The Power Delusion
You Can Make a Difference

ANTHONY CAMPOLO

It's Friday,- but Sunday's Comin'

WORD BOOKS
PUBLISHER
WACO, TEXAS

A DIVISION OF
WORD, INCORPORATED

IT'S FRIDAY, BUT SUNDAY'S COMIN'
Copyright © 1984 by Anthony Campolo.

Scripture quotations marked KJV are from the King James Version of the Bible. Quotations marked NKJV are from the New King James Version, copyright © 1979, 1980, 1982, Thomas Nelson, Inc., Publishers. Quotations marked NASB are from the New American Standard Bible, © The Lockman Foundation 1960, 1962, 1963, 1968, 1971, 1972, 1973, 1975, 1977. Quotations marked NIV are taken from The Holy Bible: New International Version © 1978 by the New York International Bible Society and used by permission of Zondervan Bible Publishers. Quotations marked RSV are from the Revised Standard Version of the Bible, copyrighted 1946, 1952, © 1971, 1973 by the Division of Christian Education of the National Council of the Churches of Christ in the U.S.A., and used by permission.

Library of Congress Cataloging in Publication Data

Campolo, Anthony.
  It's Friday, but Sunday's comin'.

  1. Christian life—1960–   . 2. Jesus Christ—
Person and offices. I. Title.
BV4501.2.C248 1984   248.4   83–25895
ISBN 0–8499–0369–6

Printed in the United States of America

To Robert and Winifred Davidson
Loving In-Laws
Who Model Christian Servanthood

CONTENTS

Contents

8

CHAPTER ONE

A Very, Very Short Statement Concerning the Purpose of This Very Short Book

I like the Bible verse in the first chapter of Romans that reads "I am not ashamed of the gospel of Christ" (1:16, KJV). That verse expresses how I feel when I consider the work and message of Jesus Christ. I am not ashamed of the Gospel of Christ because the Gospel of Christ meets every need of every human being on this planet. I hope that you will discover this. No matter what your need may happen to be, I have good news for you: Jesus can meet that need. I am not ashamed of the Gospel of Christ, because I know of no situation or predicament that human beings must face that poses problems for which Jesus does not have answers. In our day and age it seems that most people have looked everywhere but to Jesus for the satisfying of their needs and the answering of their questions. In this short book I will try to point out some ways in which Jesus meets some of the most important needs of human existence.

What I have written is drawn from material that originally was part of a motion picture entitled *It's Friday, But Sunday's Comin'*. Most of this book was originally spoken material. As you read it, I would like you to keep that fact in mind. Better still, imagine that I am talking to you rather than writing to you.

11

CHAPTER TWO

Jesus Answers Our Need for Psychological Health and Emotional Well-Being

I earn my living as a sociologist, and I can verify the fact that one of the most common tendencies these days is for troubled people to turn to psychologists and sociologists for help. More and more people believe that social science can solve their problems. If you have been caught up in this mania, I have bad news for you: the social scientific approach to problem solving is not as successful as you may think. Those who try it often find it falls short of their expectations.

The Hans Eysenck study, one of the most significant evaluative studies of the treatment of the emotionally disturbed, points out that if you have psychological problems, psychoanalysts and psychotherapists may not offer you much help. Among those who go to psychoanalysts, Eysenck reports, 44 percent become healthy in one year. Among those who go to psychotherapists, 53 percent get well within a year. Among those who go to psychiatrists about 61 percent become healthy within a year. However, among those who are emotionally troubled and seek no professional help, 73 percent get well within a year.

These results frighten me. I don't know whether the statistics surprise you as much as they surprised me, but I found myself wondering whether professional psychoanalysts and psychotherapists help people or make them worse. It appears that those whom we hope can help us when we are psychologically and emotionally disturbed seem to be keeping us sick.

How many of the people you know who go for professional counseling from psychoanalysts and therapists seem never to get out of counseling? Five or six years after they start seeing some analysts or therapists, they are still paying twenty-five dollars or more a half-hour once a week for treatment and showing very few signs of improvement. If you ask why, you might find the answer in the fact that social scientists have often tended to ignore the basic principles of the gospel.

First of all, counselors sometimes make the mistake of tracing all of our emotional and psychological difficulties to events and traumas that happened in the past. They usually try to figure out what it is in a person's background that has made that person into the kind of individual that he or she is in the present. For many counselors, the case history of the individual supposedly provides all the clues necessary to figure out the person's problems. I know several psychologists, particularly those who call themselves behaviorists, advocating what they call "behavioral modification models," who tie into this style of thinking. They are sure that humans are nothing more than socially conditioned creatures whose futures have been predetermined by their pasts. Neo-Freudian psychoanalysts are almost as bad as the behaviorists, for they too put an overemphasis on the way that the individual's past controls his destiny.

When I was a university lecturer, there was a colleague of mine who was heavily into this approach. He could be counted on to explain all personal problems as being a result of poor toilet training. I loved to sneak into his lectures and hear him explain his theories to students. He was a brilliant teacher, and I find that few things are more fun than listening to such an intelligent person articulate some stupid ideas.

With him, everything about a person was the result of toilet training. When he lectured he would make this point with all the enthusiasm and zeal of a Baptist evangelist. He would say, "Students, the first demand that society ever makes on the individual comes with toilet training. What happens in toilet training is a precursor to all the demands that society will ever make on the person. Please know that toilet training is the first thing that society requires of anyone. The mother is the communicator of societal demands. Consider how she pleads for compliance with social expectations, how she implores the child and begs, 'Do it for Mommy! Do it for Mommy!' However, the child sometimes resists the pleas of his mother. He may rebel against her wishes, and when this happens social rebellion is bred into the youngster. The child may defiantly say, 'No!' If the mother is tough and steadfast, she may demand, 'You stay there until something happens!' The child stays there. He works on it. He works on it hard. He gives to the task everything he's got and then after a long time he succeeds and finally produces the gift for which society has pled." (I must admit I never heard it called a "gift" before.)

The lecturer reached the height of absurdity when

17

he cried out to the students, "I ask you, what does society do with this gift that the child has produced on its behalf? What does it do with the results of the child's labor? Does society preserve it? Does society honor it? Does society view it as a symbol of the child's accomplishment? No! Society flushes it. There and then the child learns that what he produces for society has no lasting significance, no continual importance."

You may laugh at all of this, but this professor was serious.

Does the past really determine who we are and what we are? Do childhood processes like toilet training really predestine our future behavior? Are we nothing more than Pavlovian dogs who have been conditioned to respond to particular stimuli in a particular manner? Are we simply products of our environments and conditioning?

I think not! Furthermore, it is very important to recognize that the Gospel does not affirm such a notion. The Bible does not teach that the past determines what we are; as a matter of fact, the Bible teaches something radically different. According to the Scriptures, the future holds the clues to who we are and what we are in the present. The future, not the past, is considered to be the most important dimension of the human personality. The believer of the Bible does not remain content by asking, "Where did I come from?" For the Christian, the more important question is, "Where am I going?"

The Bible teaches that a person's past or background is not the most important thing about him or her. Rather, as the Christian knows, the most im-

18

portant thing about an individual is where that person is going and what future that individual chooses.

I have had students come into my office confused and emotionally messed up. They were floundering; they were failing; they were flunking out of school. So often, their sad circumstances were primarily the result of the fact that they were not going anywhere. They had no goals. They had no aspirations. Their lives had no purpose, and they could not imagine a desirable meaning for existence. Their futures were devoid of hope.

I discovered that if I could get such students "turned on" to some beautiful goals, if I could get them to believe that their lives could have some magnificent purpose, they would often get completely turned around and almost immediately would straighten out. I have had the thrill of watching such kids change from being lethargic and boring people into persons who have dynamic personalities, who possess wholeness of self and who are moving toward lives of joyful fulfillment. I am sure that you, out of your own experience, can cite cases of people who were confused, distraught, and emotionally unbalanced, but became happy and well-integrated persons when they made the decision to commit themselves to becoming new persons. There is a great deal of evidence to support the thesis that we are heavily dependent upon what we choose to become. This is the *Good News* (which is what the word *gospel* means). We are not predetermined creatures. We can make decisions that can modify our behavior and make us into new creatures.

Ultimately, a Christian is somebody who wants to

19

become a new person and who realizes that this is a possibility through committing his or her life to Christ and being willing to become whatever Christ wants him or her to be.

When an individual makes such a total commitment to Christ, God will send His Holy Spirit to strengthen and enable such a person to carry out that commitment. Persons who decide to become what Jesus wants them to be are empowered to become new creatures. The Bible teaches:

> Therefore, if any one is in Christ, he is a new creation; the old has passed away, behold, the new has come.
>
> *2 Corinthians 5:17*, RSV

> Beloved, we are God's children now; it does not yet appear what we shall be, but we know that when he appears we shall be like him, for we shall see him as he is.
>
> *1 John 3:2*, RSV

I want to make it clear that *I am not opposed to counselors.* The Bible clearly teaches that counseling is a gift that the Holy Spirit gives to certain people in order that they might be able to "edify" and "build up" those who need help. What concerns me is the fact that too many counselors operate on principles and assumptions about human personality that are contrary to those outlined in the Scriptures. If a counselor believes that persons can make decisions that have the potential to transform them into new creatures, I shout, "Hurrah!" But when counseling becomes

20

nothing more than an analysis of the past in the belief that insight into the factors conditioning the person's present personality will deliver him in health and happiness, I object.

I am not suggesting that the past does not *influence* who a person is. I am only suggesting that the past does not *determine* who a person is. I am convinced that the past influences the options from which an individual can choose his or her destiny. Obviously, the background and personal history of an individual limit what any one of us becomes. But no matter what our backgrounds happen to be, we all have options. There are always alternatives from which we can choose. Ultimately, we are deciding creatures to whom God has given the freedom to will our futures.

Most people who go to counselors already know what they must do to straighten out their lives. The counselor can help such persons to see their options more clearly, but in the end the good counselor will make the individual aware that he/she alone has the capability of making the decisions that will transform despair into hope, sadness into joy, and confusion into peace.

For instance, when a man comes into my office and cries, "Oh, Dr. Campolo, I do not know what to do. My life is such a mess," I ask, as professionally as I know how, "What's the matter? What's happened?"

He responds, "I am married to a lovely wife, but at the same time I am sexually involved with my secretary. I love them both, and I don't think that there is any way out of this predicament. I am living in hell."

I respond by saying, "That's not a difficult problem

21

to solve. You have three options. The first option is that you can get rid of your secretary and stick with your wife."

"I can't do that," he says.

"Okay," I respond, "you can get rid of your wife and marry your secretary."

"I can't do that either," he says.

"Okay," I respond, "you can get rid of your wife *and* your secretary and you can start over again from scratch."

"No! no!" he says, "you don't understand!"

"No, *you* don't understand!" I reply. "You have only three options. We can go on talking from now until the Kingdom comes about how your rotten childhood set up these kinds of problems. We can talk about how poor toilet training created your unhappy psyche. But none of this talk will solve your problem. You have a decision to make, and the sooner you make it the sooner you will find peace and deliverance from your anxiety. Furthermore, out of the three options that I outlined for you, there is only one option that will work, and that is to get rid of your secretary and stay with your wife. If you choose to do other than that, you will not be doing what God requires of you, and you are going to be messed up the rest of your life. You have to make a decision before you walk out of this room, and if you refuse to decide, you will have indirectly decided to remain a messed-up person."

This kind of tough talk may seem "unprofessional," but it is about time that we stop playing little games with people and realize that one of the main reasons they are sick is because they cannot bring themselves to make decisions. More specifically, they are unwilling to choose to do the things that they know Jesus would have them do. They are not willing to be what Jesus wants them to be.

That may be your problem today. You may be psychologically or emotionally messed up simply because you refuse to decide to do what you know Jesus expects of you. Your problem may lie in the fact that you have been fooled into thinking there is some alternative to God's will that will allow you to be happy. Perhaps you need to realize that when the time comes that you choose to live according to the will of God, then all things will begin to work together for good (Rom. 8:28). Perhaps you ought to recognize that when you decide about the future, you have delivered yourself from being a victim of the past. God allows you the freedom to decide your destiny and therefore gives to you the ability to transform your present. You must make some ultimate decisions. The future must be decided not only for this life, but for the life to come. What will your decisions be? I hope you will say with Joshua, "As for me and my house, we will serve the Lord" (Josh. 24:15, KJV). If you decide for the Lord and choose to live according to His will, you will have taken a major stride toward psychological and emotional well-being.

CHAPTER THREE

*Jesus Satisfies
Our Need
for a
Sense of Self-Worth
and Value*

Among the many decisions you must make that will determine who and what you are, is the decision as to who will be the most important person in your life. We seldom realize that who we are and what we become are, to a great extent, influenced by whom we choose to make the most important persons in our respective lives.

Charles H. Cooley, one of the most important modern social scientists and a dean of American sociology, developed the concept of the "looking-glass self." Anyone who has taken even an elementary course in sociology has been introduced to this primary concept of human understanding. Cooley's postulate goes like this: a person's self-concept is established by what he/she thinks the most important persons in his/her life think of him/her.

For instance, if I believe that the most important person in my life thinks that I am the best-looking guy in town, it won't be long before I begin to think that I *am* the best-looking guy in town. That may be hard for many of you to believe since I have a double chin and I am bald. But to all of you who are not bald, I say that they do not put marble tops on cheap furniture. Furthermore, I would like to point out that when we were born, we were all given so many hormones, and if some of you guys want to use yours to grow hair, that's your business. It doesn't make much difference if you and the rest of my audience do not think I am good-looking, because my wife does, and she is far more important to me than any of you or anybody else who reads this book. She influences what I think of myself more than what I think you think of me.

In our earliest years, our mothers are probably the most important people in our lives. Hence our self-concept and sense of personal worth is usually determined by what we think our mothers think of us.

I grew up in West Philadelphia where I was pretty much in the minority, since I am Italian and in West Philadelphia most of the people were either Jews or blacks. Consequently, I was the left-out kid. My earliest recollections about my neighborhood involve the ways in which the Jewish kids always amazed me. They were so successful and self-confident. You may argue to the contrary, but I tell you that Jewish kids are the smartest of them all. The way things seemed to me back then, there was no question about it. Jewish kids were the most successful at school.

Even in adulthood Jewish people seem to be better achievers and academicians than the rest of us. They produce more Nobel Prize winners per capita than any other ethnic group. They are bright people in every way. They seem to be at the top of every profession. If you want to look for the reason for this success and achievement, I urge you to give special consideration to Jewish mothers. Jewish mothers have been

the brunt of a lot of bad jokes. They have been called
pushy, domineering, and a number of other unflatter-
ing things. But I do not buy these judgments. I think
that Jewish mothers are among the best mothers.
Their cultural background has trained them to help
their children maximize their potentialities. Jewish
mothers are terrific. Their culture has built into moth-
erhood the idea that the primary responsibility of a
mother is to build up her child and make the child
feel special. Consequently, Jewish kids grow up thinking that they are wonderful.

There was a Jewish kid named Albert Finkelstein
who lived in my neighborhood. He usually stopped
by to pick me up on the way to school. One day when
we were leaving my house he said, "You know the
difference between my mother and your mother?
When we leave my house, my mother says, 'Albert,
do you have your books?' and when we leave your
house, your mother always says, 'Tony, do you have
your lunch?' "

That's the difference. We Italians get fatter and the
Jewish people get smarter.

The typical Jewish kid grows up being told by his/
her mother that he/she is bright, handsome, and capable of doing great things. That kid can go off and
flunk the first grade; it does not make any difference
or change her opinion. The Jewish mother shrugs
her shoulders and says, "It just goes to show—they
don't know how to educate a genius down there at
that school."

Because the Jewish mother thinks that her child is
bright and beautiful, her child will pick up that opinion. Consequently, the child will begin to think of

29

himself/herself as his/her mother does and will begin to define himself/herself as bright and beautiful.

The effect of the positive self-image created by the Jewish mother goes even further. According to the expectations of most social scientists, the child probably *will become* what he/she thinks he/she is. Some psychologists call this a "self-fulfilling prophecy." That means that if the child thinks that he/she is bright and capable of great things he/she probably will become a bright person who does great things. If this is true, it is little wonder that Jewish kids so often grow up to achieve great things. They are simply living up to the positive self-images that have been created for them by their parents.

I think it would be wonderful if all mothers took a page from the Jewish mother's handbook on child-rearing and made their children feel great about themselves. Unfortunately, too many parents ruin their children and keep them from realizing their potentialities because they constantly put them down, criticizing them in such a way as to make them feel worthless. Some parents are afraid that if they praise their children, the children will become swelled-headed egotists. They think that they can elicit greater accomplishments from their children if they withhold approval for their work. Unfortunately, they withhold the affirmation and praise that is so essential for building positive self-images for their children. Almost everywhere I go, I meet people who have lousy self-concepts because their parents failed to build them up to believe that they were beautiful people who were capable of great things.

The principle of Cooley's "looking-glass self" is

at work during every stage of life. It does not cease to operate when we become teenagers and adults. A young man in my church went to play basketball under one of the great coaches of America. I was very interested in finding out what it was about this particular coach that made him so special and enabled him to turn out so many championship teams. I asked the young man what it was like to play under the direction of this legendary sports figure.

My friend said, "It was incredible playing for him. He constantly worked on getting all of his players to feel good about themselves. During the game he seemed to pay more attention to those who were riding the bench than to those who were playing. He was always talking to us bench-warmers and telling us how important we were and what great players we were. Every time a shot would be missed he would nudge me and say, 'If you were in there, you would have made that shot!' A pass would go astray and he would say, 'You would never blow a pass like that.' A play would get messed up, and he would yell, 'Oh, how we need a player like you in this game. That's what we need, we need someone like you out there.' He would go on like that throughout the entire game. By the time the game was over, I felt so terrific that it never occurred to me to ask, 'Coach, if I am so great, why don't you put me in?' "

My friend went on to say, "I remember the first time I took the court in a varsity game. It was against Michigan State. I wondered whether I'd be too nervous to play and too scared to function. But when I walked onto the court at East Lansing, I felt only one emotion. It was pity. I pitied the players at Michi-

31

gan State. Our coach had made me and the others so confident about ourselves and so convinced that we were the greatest players ever to set foot on the basketball court, that we knew the Michigan State team would be blown away. I realized that those poor Michigan players had invited their mothers and girlfriends to the game, and here we were, about to destroy them. My feelings were justified; we did just that. We beat Michigan State soundly. I played well and with confidence. I believe it was all because my coach made me believe that I was a great player, and it seemed natural to me to play well."

This is just another example of how a person's self-concept and his/her ability to perform successfully is influenced by what he/she thinks the most important person in his/her life thinks of him/her. The positive self-image that the person develops in his/her relationship to the one who is most significant in his/her life can have fantastic positive effects. However, it is easy to point to instances in which the self-image that an individual picked up from the person he deemed most important in his life was not a good one. And the effects of a poor self-image can be devastating.

One day I was on a beach with my wife, a friend, and his wife. While we were sitting visiting with each other, a young woman dressed in a bikini walked by. My friend looked at her, nudged me, and said, "Hey, Tony, look at that! Now that's really something!"

I resisted a strong desire to punch him in the mouth. I was angry at this remark about that woman who was twenty years younger than he was. I felt that when

32

he said, "That's really something," he was indirectly
saying to his forty-year-old wife, "You're nothing."

You might argue that his wife probably would not
take the remark that way, to which I respond by asking,
"Why shouldn't she?" I wonder how most husbands
would feel if every time some young, well-built guy
walked down the street their wives would nudge them
and say, "Oh, wow, look at that, look at that! I wish
I had a guy that was built like that!" I think that most
of them would be furious. I do not think that we chau-
vinistic males could handle that kind of put-down.

Incidentally, I am convinced that these not-too-
subtle put-downs are responsible for much of the
adultery that occurs in our society. If a husband puts
down his wife and makes her feel like an unattractive
and uninteresting nincompoop, she becomes easy to
seduce. All that is necessary for her to fall into a de-
structive sexual liaison is for some other man to come
along who will build her up and tell her that she is
special, intelligent, and alluring. Because of her desire
to establish self-worth, she is likely to gravitate to
this other man who provides a positive self-image.
She can easily become the victim in an adulterous
relationship.

Building up one another is a God-given responsibility. The Scripture admonishes us to enter into a minis-
try of "edification," or uplifting. That means when
people are down we are supposed to pick them up.
When they feel like nothing we are supposed to make
them feel like something special. When they feel
worthless we are supposed to make them feel infinitely
precious.

Few characters in the Bible inspire me as much

33

as Barnabas. His name means "Son of Encouragement," and surely this name suited him well. He is mentioned only three times in the Scriptures, and on each occasion he is providing encouragement and support for others. He seems to be constantly at work making people feel good about themselves and enabling them to believe in themselves.

First, we find him selling his property in order to help the church carry out its mission. He so believed in what the church was about that he was willing to sacrifice everything he had in order to encourage it to fulfill its mission. There was no question that Barnabas believed in the church. Consequently, the church was able to believe in itself.

Second, I find that Barnabas helped Paul gain acceptance in the Christian fellowship. For years Paul had been the leader of the persecution of the church. It could be justifiably said that the church looked upon Paul as its most prominent enemy. Therefore, when Paul underwent his dramatic conversion and sought to become part of the fellowship of believers, those in the church greeted the news with a high level of suspicion. They were understandably cautious when it came to receiving their former enemy as a Christian brother. Many of them must have wondered if Paul was not simply using the pretense of a conversion so that he might gain entrance into the body of believers in order to spy on them. They must have wondered whether this man would identify them to the ruling authorities and mark them for martyrdom. But when nobody else believed in Paul, Barnabas did. When nobody else saw the potentialities in Paul, Barnabas did. We all must wonder whether Paul ever would

34

have become the great and self-confident leader that he did, if Barnabas had not encouraged him and believed in him and thus made it possible for Paul to believe in himself.

The third time we find reference to Barnabas in the Scriptures, we discover him helping a broken, discouraged, and humble John Mark out of a state of self-contempt and encouraging him to achieve greatness.

On the first missionary journey, Paul, Barnabas, and John Mark set out from Antioch to preach the Gospel across the face of the then-known world. Things became very difficult; there was tremendous persecution. There were shipwrecks; there was disease; there was so much trouble that finally John Mark gave up. He couldn't handle it; he chickened out and returned to Antioch a humiliated failure. In every way John Mark was a defeated person.

When Paul and Barnabas later returned to Antioch, John Mark asked for a second chance. He pled with his Christian brothers and explained that he was truly repentant for what he had done. He promised to be more resolute in the future. We can almost hear him: "Please, Paul, give me another chance. Take me on the next missionary journey. Give me one more opportunity. I promise I won't fail you." But Paul wouldn't do it. The same man who could write, "If someone is caught in a sin, you who are spiritual should restore him gently; but watch yourself, or you also may be tempted" (Gal. 6:1, NIV) refused the pleadings of the young John Mark. In this particular case we would have to say that Paul did not practice what he preached. Thank God that Barnabas did. I

35

can just see him putting his arm around John Mark and saying, "Come on, don't listen to him. Paul has a nasty streak in him. I know that you have a great future in the work of God's Kingdom and I believe that God is going to do great things through you. If Paul won't take you on the next missionary journey, you and I will go together and he can take this new fellow Silas with him."

And so it was; Paul took Silas, and Barnabas took John Mark. They went their separate ways. Barnabas and John Mark had a splendid missionary outreach. Church historians say wonderful things about them. But perhaps what is most important is that John Mark later wrote for us one of the four Gospels. None of that could have happened had not Barnabas been the Son of Encouragement. Mark would have been lost to the work of the church if Barnabas had not enabled him to believe in himself and to regain a sense of self-worth.

When the Scripture speaks of Barnabas, it tells us, "He was a good man, full of the Holy Spirit and faith; and a great number of people were brought to the Lord" (Acts 11:24, NIV). Isn't that a beautiful epitaph? Wouldn't you like to have that written on your tombstone when you are laid to rest? There is no reason why those words shouldn't be on your tombstone. God has called you to be what Barnabas was—a son or a daughter of encouragement, a person who creates in others the ability for them to believe in themselves. God wants you to be the kind of person who makes everybody that you meet feel gloriously wonderful, self-assured, and precious.

You may say to me, "Tony, I'm quite willing to

be a Barnabas for others, but first of all I need somebody to be a Barnabas to me. I have nobody to pick me up and make me feel good about myself. There is no one in my life who really believes in me and makes me feel special."

To that I can only respond by telling you to make Jesus the most important person in your life. Remember, your self-concept ultimately will be determined by what you think the most important person in your life thinks of you, and if you allow Jesus to become the most important person in your life, you will probably develop a very positive self-image.

Jesus teaches that you should love Him more than you love your mother and your father. He expects you to regard Him with such importance and love that no other relationship will be able to compare with that which you have with Him. You must be willing to say in the depths of your being that He will have preeminence over all others. You must be willing to say, "For me, to live is Christ and to die is gain" (Phil. 1:21, NIV). He will pick you up when you are down. He believes in you. He wants to make you feel special.

To say "I believe in Jesus" is not enough. You must be willing to acknowledge Him as the most important person in your life. You must be willing to say, "I will do what He wants me to do above all else and above any demands that others may place upon me."

37

If you will make that decision, I have great news for you—I can promise you a very positive self-image. When Jesus is the most important person in your life, you will soon come to define yourself in the same way that Jesus defines you. You will begin to think of yourself as He thinks of you. And here's more good news: Jesus thinks you're great! He thinks you're terrific. He really does.

You say, "Not me, Tony. You don't know me or the sin in my life. There are things that I can never tell you. If you knew them it would cause you to view me with contempt."

We could compare horror stories. You could tell me how rotten you are and I could tell you how rotten I am and we could try to see which of us is worse. Both of us would end up in despair. But that's not what Jesus wants us to do. He wants us to realize that once we accept Him as our Savior and Lord, we stand before Him as perfect people. That's right! When Jesus looks at me, He doesn't see anything wrong with me at all. In the words of Scripture, I'm "clothed in His righteousness." The Bible says that my sin is blotted out. It is buried in the deepest sea; it is remembered no more.

Just the other day I was reading through the Book of Hebrews and several times I came upon that phrase, "Your sin is remembered no more." On the cross, Jesus took your sin and my sin and said, "It's mine." There on Calvary, says the Scripture, "He who knew no sin became sin for our sakes." If there is any under-preached doctrine in the New Testament it is the forgetfulness of God. God forgets. He not only sent His Son to be punished for our sins. He not only forgives us our sins because of what His Son did on Calvary, but God forgets the sins that we have committed.

I am so glad that my sins are not remembered. I would hate to go to heaven if they were, wouldn't you? I can just imagine approaching the judgment seat of the Lord and the Lord saying to me, "Campolo, we've been waiting for you. Peter! Get the Campolo book," and Peter saying, "Lord, we don't have a book, we have a library on this guy." I don't know if they do have a Campolo book in heaven, but if they do and if someday they open it up, only good stuff is going to be recorded there. If you ask about all of the bad things that I've done, I can only tell you again, they are blotted out, buried in the deepest sea, remembered no more. Now that's good news and it's true for you too. If you will allow Jesus to be your Savior, He will take your sins upon Himself and endure the punishment for them. He will forgive you and He will forget that you ever sinned at all.

When I was a kid in daily vacation Bible school, the teacher taught us the meaning of the word "justification." She explained to me that justification meant just-as-if-I-never-sinned! Years have gone by since that simple Bible lesson. I have read a host of books, studied the Bible in the original languages and explored the meaning of that word in discussions with theologians. But after it is all said and done, I must admit that nothing I have ever heard has improved on that Bible school teacher's simple statement.

If Jesus is the most important person in your life, you are justified. That means standing before God just as if you have never sinned. That is the incredible good news I want you to grasp.

39

What is more is that Jesus not only sees you as justified; he also sees you as one having tremendous potentiality. You may not think that you can become much, but He does. You may not think of yourself as special, but He does. To use biblical language, through Him you can become exceedingly more than you could ever hope or think. He has great expectations for you and He knows that you are destined for greatness. He has given you gifts that you don't even know you have. He believes that you can achieve more than your wildest imagination could ever comprehend. The One who created the universe thinks you're terrific. He believes that you are so precious that as far as He is concerned, if you were the only person who ever lived and no one came after you, He would have been willing to die just for you.

I don't know what they are doing in heaven, but I think that God must be acting like a proud grandmother. He's probably got a wallet with your picture in it and when ever He is talking with the archangels He probably weaves talk about you into the conversation. I can just imagine Him whipping out His wallet, showing the angels your picture, and saying, "Isn't my child beautiful? Isn't my child wonderful? You know, I think my child is going to grow up and do great things in the world." Whenever I meet somebody who has an inferiority complex, I know that that person does not live in a close personal relationship with Jesus. How can anybody believe that he is inferior or worthless when the King of kings and Lord of lords has declared that person to be infinitely precious in His sight? Whenever somebody puts himself/herself down and says, "God doesn't love me," I feel like yelling, "Who do you think you are? What makes you think that you're different from the rest of us? If God loves every single human being infinitely then He loves you infinitely. You have no right to say, 'I'm the exception.' " Furthermore, it is arrogant to say

40

that what I have done and what I am is greater than God's capacity to love. All I can say is, "No way. God loves infinitely and to the uttermost. He loves you and believes in you even if you refuse to accept these truths."

Some people in the church confuse having humility with having an inferiority complex. God expects us to be humble, not to have an inferiority complex. A person who is continually saying, "I'm no good; there is so much sin in my life that the Lord could never use me because I have not achieved the level of spirituality that is necessary to be a true servant of the Lord," always comes out looking religious even if it is in a phony way. He seems to be saying, "See how humble I am?"

I feel like saying in response, "You seem very proud of your humility."

God does not want us playing such manipulative games. He calls upon us to affirm our identities as His children. He wants us to acknowledge our infinite worth to Him.

Fred Craddock, a professor at Phillips Theological Seminary, tells the story of an encounter that made a profound impression on him and provides us with a powerful illustration of the way a person's self-definition can change when he or she realizes that he/she is a child of God.

Professor Craddock was vacationing in Gatlinburg, Tennessee. He and his wife were seated at a table in a restaurant when an old man came up to them and asked, "How are you doing? Are you having a good time? Are you on vacation?"

"Yes," said Professor Craddock, "we are on vacation, and yes, we are having a good time."

41

"What do you do for a living?" the old man asked.

Professor Craddock, wanting to get rid of the old man and return to the private conversation he was having with his wife, answered, "I'm a professor of homiletics." He was sure that a title like that would drive off the unwelcomed intruder. But it didn't.

"Oh, you're a preacher," the old man said. "Let me tell you a preacher story."

It seems as if everybody has a preacher story, and Professor Craddock did not want to hear another one. But before he could do anything, the old man had drawn up a chair to the table and started to unwind his tale. He said, "I was born an illegitimate child. I never knew who my father was and that was very hard on me. The boys at school had names they called me, and they made fun of me. When I walked down the main street of our little town, I felt that people were staring at me and asking that terrible question, 'I wonder who the father of that boy is?' I spent a lot of time by myself and I didn't have any friends. One day a new preacher came to town and everybody was talking about how good he was. I had never gone to church before, but one Sunday I thought I would go to hear him preach. He was a good preacher. I kept going back. Each time I would go late and leave early so I wouldn't have to talk to anybody. Then one Sunday I got so caught up in the preacher's message I forgot to leave, and before I knew what was happening, he had said the benediction and the service was over. I tried to get out of the church, but people had already filled the aisles and I couldn't get past them. Suddenly, I felt a heavy hand on my shoulder. When I turned, that big tall preacher was looking down at me and asking, 'What's your name, boy? Whose son are you?' I just shook when he asked that question. But before I could say anything, he said, 'I know who you are. I know who your family is. There's a distinct family resemblance. Why, you're the son—you're the son—you're the son of God!' You know, mister, those words changed my life."

The old man got up and left, and a waitress came over and asked, "You know who that was?"

"No," answered Professor Craddock.

"That's Ben Hooper. Two-term governor of Tennessee."

A man learned that he was the son of God, and it changed the whole way in which he viewed himself. The opinions of others could no longer diminish his sense of dignity and worth. I wish that everyone would come to an awareness that he or she is a true child of God and an heir to the King of kings.

> But as many as received Him, to them He gave the right to become the children of God, even to those who believe in His name.
>
> *John 1:12*, NKJV

> [We are] heirs of God and joint heirs with Christ.
> *Romans 8:17*, NKJV

43

If you can grasp these truths and apply them to your life, you will never have a poor self-image again.

I am not ashamed of the Gospel of Christ, because it fulfills my need for a positive self-image. And if you give Jesus a chance, the same will be true of you.

He is not a God of put-downs. He is a God who lifts us up and places our feet on solid rock, who teaches us to hold our heads high and calls to us with a voice that reverberates to the far corners of the universe, "You are great in My eyes."

CHAPTER FOUR

Jesus Answers
Our Need
for
Love

Everybody knows that we need love. No one doubts that having and giving love is basic to a fulfilling life. However, not enough people are aware of the fact that our society has a messed-up view of love. The popular culture, particularly as it is expressed in television and motion pictures, projects a view of sentimental romance that tries to convince the American population that romance is what love is all about. In reality, when romance is carefully analyzed, it becomes clear that it is so distinct from love that it is questionable whether we should even consider romance to be a form of love.

Romance is self-centered and egoistic. If you need any proof of that, just look to the lyrics of popular love songs. Those lyrics will give you all of the evidence you need to make the case for the self-centeredness of romance. Listen to them as they come across the radio waves or via the stereo. Listen carefully as the rock "artist" mumbles, "I need you—I want you—I can't get along without you, baby." The whole emphasis of the song is on the "I." The frequency with which the words "I" and "me" occur is convincing evidence that the whole emotion that is being described is nothing but an ego trip. At first glance it

47

may seem likely that the other person is important, when in reality it is the ego gratification of the lover that is preeminent in the lyrics of popular songs.

In reviewing my own personal life I can reflect upon the egocentricity of my romantic relationships. When I was a student in college, I went steady with a girl for about a year and a half. After that time she had had enough of me, and decided to give me the "shaft." Since it was a Christian college, I guess I will have to refer to it as the "holy shaft." I was upset, to say the least, less because I had lost her than because it had been a blow to my ego. She told me it was all over and I can remember saying to her, "You can't do this to me. I need you, I want you, my life would be meaningless without you."

She responded in an unconcerned manner, "Gee, that's a shame."

I deserved that response. After all, the only reason that I gave her to stay with me was to serve my own self-interest.

I needed her. *I* wanted her. *I* was concerned about what she was doing to *me.* In none of my romantic mumblings had I said anything that expressed a concern for her. That is the nature of romance; it is self-centered. That is why one prominent writer in the field of love and romance contends that romance should not even be called love. In her book *Love and Limerence,** Dorothy Tennov says we should use the word "limerence" rather than "love" when referring to romance. She argues that limerence is such an overpowering emotion that it can render an individ-

48

---

* Briarcliff Manor, NY: Stein and Day, 1979.

ual incapable of functioning. It can leave a person psychologically disoriented, devoid of the power to concentrate, and in total emotional disarray. Just because it is a powerful emotion does not mean that romance should be called love. Tennov says that love is qualitatively different from limerence or romance.

According to 1 Corinthians 13, love has none of the self-centered characteristics of romance:

> Love is patient and kind; love is not jealous or boastful; it is not arrogant or rude. Love does not insist on its own way; it is not irritable or resentful; it does not rejoice at wrong, but rejoices in the right. Love bears all things, believes all things, hopes all things, endures all things. Love never ends. As for prophecies, they will pass away; as for tongues, they will cease; as for knowledge, it will pass away.
>
> *1 Corinthians 13:4–8,* RSV

Outside of religious literature I have found many other statements that contrast love with romance. One of the best comes from a children's story written by Marjorie Williams. I read a lot of children's stories, probably because I don't understand big people's stories. *The Velveteen Rabbit* has to be my favorite. At one point in the story there is an intriguing discussion between a toy rabbit and a toy horse. The toy horse's description of a love relationship is so powerful that it makes romance seem superficial by comparison.

49

> "What is Real?" asked the Rabbit one day, when they were lying side by side near the nursery fender, before Nana came to tidy the room. "Does it mean having things that buzz inside of you and a stick-out handle?"
>
> "Real isn't how you are made," said the Skin Horse.

"It's a thing that happens to you. When a child loves you for a long, long time, not just to play with, but REALLY loves you, then you become Real."

"Does it hurt?" asked the Rabbit.

"Sometimes," said the Skin Horse, for he was always truthful. "When you are Real you don't mind being hurt."

"Does it happen all at once, like being wound up," he asked, "or bit by bit?"

"It doesn't happen all at once," said the Skin Horse. "You become. It takes a long time. That's why it doesn't often happen to people who break easily, or have sharp edges, or have to be carefully kept. Generally, by the time you are Real, most of your hair has been loved off, and your eyes drop out and you get loose in the joints and very shabby. But these things don't matter at all, because once you are Real you can't be ugly, except to people who don't understand."

I, like so many other Americans, grew up unaware of the distinction between love and romance. I believed, like Ezio Pinza in the musical *South Pacific*, that "some enchanted evening [I would] meet a stranger across a crowded room, and somehow [I would] know . . ." Consequently, I spent most of my adolescent years looking across crowded rooms. I was just one more American who had bought into the romantic syndrome and lost the opportunity to appreciate the meaning of love.

The first problem with romance is that it is not very stable. A normal person has at least six romantic experiences prior to marriage. Most of us have one romantic turn-on after the other. These ecstatic excursions that make our heads spin, our stomachs ache, and our knees buckle, are an expected part of growing up. Granted, there are a few people who have one great romantic experience and contend that it lasts for a lifetime. But such persons are few and far between. They are much more rare than we romantic Americans want to admit. Generally, we are people who fall in and out of love relationships until we hit that age when society says we ought to be married. In the United States that age for males is about twenty-three years; for women it is about twenty-one years. Usually what happens is that people marry whomever they happen to be romantically involved with at those socially prescribed ages for marriage.

This leaves most married people asking me the question, "Are you suggesting that if I had waited ten years I might have married someone other than the person I did marry?"

In all probability—yes! In those ten years you would have fallen in and out of romantic relationships with several potential partners. Without the experience of living together as marital partners you and your mate would have developed and changed so differently that you probably would not even have been attracted to each other if you had met a decade later.

Once you are married, romance often shows signs of rapid decline. According to research done by sociologists W. F. Nimkoff and Arthur L. Wood, romance diminishes about 80 percent in intensity during the first two years of marriage. We don't like to hear that kind of thing, and when I make such a statement, people often cry out, "Not true! Not true!" But it is true, even if most people refuse to admit it.

Although it happened more than twenty-five years

51

ago, I remember saying to my prospective bride three weeks before the wedding, "Just think, Peg, three more weeks and we are going to share everything. We'll share the beautiful things; we'll share the ugly things. We'll share the hard things; we'll share the easy things. We'll share all of life together."

After twenty-five years of marriage I have to admit that when my kid vomits at three o'clock in the morning and my wife is cleaning up the mess, I have no desire to *share* with her. I don't know about you, but I usually roll over in bed and pretend that I am still sleeping. In the morning my wife exclaims, "Bart was sick last night!" I respond with pretended surprise, "Oh, really?" I suspect my wife pulls the same thing on me when I'm the one who gets up to handle the mess.

There is another story that I can tell that will give evidence of my declining romanticism. (I must admit that it is one of my favorites.) One night our family was coming home to Pennsylvania from New Jersey. We were crossing the Walt Whitman bridge into Philadelphia when suddenly my wife, who had been sitting quietly next to me, pathetically cried out, "Look at us! Look at us!"

"I'm looking!" I responded. "What's the matter?"

She said, "Look where you're sitting!"

"I'm driving the car," I answered. "When I'm driving the car, I find it best to sit behind the wheel. What's bothering you?"

She pointed into the car in front of us and said, "Look at them! *Look at them!*"

I looked into the car in front of us and saw that

the driver seemed to have two heads, and I knew
what my wife was thinking. I didn't say another word,
but crossed the bridge, entered Philadelphia, and
drove along the Schuylkill River until I found a place
to park the car in one of those special spots designated
for lovers. It was right on the edge of the river bank.
The other cars that were there were undoubtedly oc-
cupied by people who were "making out." (There
was no way to tell because the windows of those cars
were all steamed up.) Our kids were still asleep in
the back seat. I locked the car doors, turned off the
ignition, put on the parking lights, reached out and
grabbed my wife. As I pulled her toward me, I turned
her sideways so as to cradle her in my arms. Unfortunately, in the process I smashed her head on the steer-
ing wheel.

"What are you doing?" she asked.

I said, "I'm being romantic."

"Take me home," she responded with disgust.

"I can't win," I said in dismay. "If I'm not romantic
you cry, and if I do get romantic you get disgusted."

Don't get me wrong. Just because I'm not the
sweep-her-off-her-feet type does not mean that I'm
not in love. Quite the opposite. I am more in love
with her today than I was the day that I married her.
Furthermore, I have to question seriously whether I
actually *did* love her the day that I married her. Oh,
I was romantically turned on when she came down
the aisle to greet me at the altar. But now I have to
question whether or not *all* of those romantic feelings
were love.

It's not that I don't understand romance or fail to

53

appreciate its wonder and excitement. It is simply that I want to affirm that love goes far deeper than romance. Furthermore, the biblical language establishes this difference. It has several distinct words for love, and each of them connotes a different emotional experience. Coming closest to our concept of romance is the Greek word *eros*. It is the word from which we get our English word "erotic." The second Greek word for love is the word *philos*. This second kind of love is what grows up between two people who are committed to the same goals and purposes in life. It is what emerges between people who share common beliefs and concerns. It is a love that comes into being between two people who establish a common commitment for their lives. The third kind of love that the Greeks talked about is *agapē*. This is a special love that creates value in the object of love. It would be worthwhile for us to analyze the two latter types of love in some detail.

Plato, the ancient Greek philosopher, had some interesting things to say about love that can help us understand the meaning of *philos*. He asked us to imagine a triangle. Along the base of that imaginary triangle Plato asked that we arrange all the things in life that we think to be significant and important. As the base of the triangle is moved toward the apex, he said, the base will get smaller and smaller, leaving room for fewer and fewer things. We will drop those things which are the least important to us and we will hold onto those things which we deem to be the most important. Finally, when the apex of the triangle is reached, there is room for only one thing. Plato asked the question: "What is that one thing that you will hold onto after you have sacrificed all else?"

If you are a Christian, you will have to answer, "Jesus!" To be a Christian is not simply to believe in Jesus. It is to be able to say, "This one thing I do: setting aside all else I will give myself to Jesus; I will hold onto Him, even if all else must be sacrificed."

Whenever such a declaration of faith is made, those who do not understand the nature of the Christian commitment will ask, "What about your husband?" or, "What about your wife?" My response is that a Christian always puts Christ first. That is what it means to *be* a Christian. That is why Jesus told His disciples, "Unless you love Me more than your mother and father, your sister and brother, you are not worthy of Me."

To those who think that this is an immoral or unjust requirement, I can only point out that a person will make a better husband or a better wife if Jesus is put first. Those who have lived out a Christian life know that a commitment to Christ inevitably makes a person into a better lover. If a husband is committed to Christ and he is moving closer to Christ every day and the wife is committed to Christ and likewise is moving closer and closer to the Lord daily, then they will move, inevitably, closer and closer to each other. If two people have the same ultimate goal in life and are committed to the same ultimate reality; if both give Christ preeminence in their respective lives and move towards Him, they will move closer and closer to each other.

55

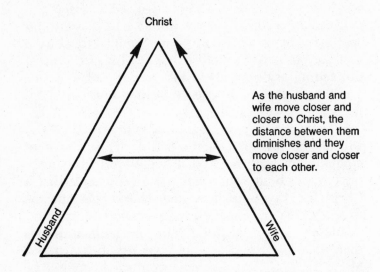

Christ

As the husband and wife move closer and closer to Christ, the distance between them diminishes and they move closer and closer to each other.

Husband

Wife

It is for this reason that the Bible requires that Christians only marry other Christians. The biblical admonition is, "Be ye not unequally yoked together with unbelievers. . . . For what fellowship hath light with darkness?" (2 Cor. 6:14, KJV).

When the Apostle Paul set down this admonition, he was not being bigoted or narrow-minded. He was simply going on the premise that *philos* never grows up between persons who do not share a common commitment. If one person is committed to Christ and the other is not, they will not grow in *philos*. Instead, they will grow apart from each other. Not sharing the same commitment, they will become increasingly alienated as the years go by. Each will carve out a lifestyle, distinct and individualistic. While they might

have been romantically involved, they will never develop the kind of intimacy that is promised in *philos.*
One contemporary philosopher, describing such a relationship, said, "He liked to walk alone. She liked to walk alone. They got married and they walked alone together."

If you think that walking alone together is impossible, look around. You will see a host of couples walking alone together. You will see countless marriages in which the wife has her interests and her commitments and the husband has interests that are completely different. They never argue; they never fight. That's because they have nothing to argue and fight about. Each of them lives in a different world. People who live in different worlds do not have points of conflict, or contention. Arguments are not necessarily a sign that a marriage is in trouble. As a matter of fact, quarreling often occurs between people who share common goals and commitments and have the same ultimate concerns. Their intensive involvement in the same thing inevitably leads to friction.

The absence of love is more often marked by indifference than it is by conflict. Indifference results when people do not have the same commitments or interests. If a marriage is going to have *philos,* then both parties must be oriented to the same goals.

Let me strongly affirm the Pauline doctrine that if you are a Christian you dare not marry anyone who does not share your commitment with Christ. If you are a Christian, you must marry only another Christian.

Incidentally, I must point out that just because somebody belongs to the same denomination that you do, or to some other Christian denomination, that does not necessarily mean that he or she is a Christian. Billy Graham rightly suggests that more than half of the people who presently hold church membership have never made commitments to Christ and cannot justifiably be called Christians. If you are a Christian, you must make sure that your potential mate is really a Christian and not simply a church member. However, if one is fortunate enough to link up with someone who shares his/her convictions, there are possibilities for a love that goes far beyond the romance of our culture. There is hope for *philos*.

Bryn Mawr College, located near my home, is an academically select women's school. On several occasions I have been invited to give special lectures there. They like me at Bryn Mawr because I am an ardent feminist. My commitment to feminism goes over big with those very bright women because they, like most people, enjoy hearing from those with whom they agree.

At Bryn Mawr, I was once asked to give a critique of traditional marriage. I was asked to evaluate the functionality of the institution in the context of our modern industrial society. Contrary to the expectations of many in the audience, I expressed strong support for traditional family values, especially as they are legitimated in Scripture. When I finished, some

of the bright young women who had come to hear me started to argue with me. They were so intelligent and articulate that I soon realized they were overwhelming me. There was no doubt that they were beating me in the argument and cutting me to intellectual smithereens.

Their contention was that romance was the ultimate basis for sexual relations and marriage. They believed that when romance dies, it is best to end the relationship lest the persons be dehumanized by living in what they referred to as "empty-shell marriages." As they refused to accept my *a priori* assumptions about Scripture, I was having a difficult time convincing them of my views. Just when I was about to go under and·experience total defeat, I remembered a story that turned the argument in my favor. This story had been told by a friend of mine who was a faculty member at a prominent theological seminary. I once heard him tell, with brilliance and in great detail, the events surrounding his mother's death after fifty-five years of marriage. He told me how she had come down for breakfast, finished eating and then suddenly slumped unconscious in her chair. Her husband rushed to her side, gathered up his bride in his arms and went running out of the house. Everyone else seemed to be frozen with shock and fear. Their neighbors all knew that something terrible had happened when they saw this old man set his wife in the front seat of his pickup truck, pull out of his driveway and take off down the highway like a teenager starting off in a hot rod race. When he got her to the hospital, she was pronounced dead on arrival.

On the day of the funeral they went out to the cemetery in the late afternoon and buried her in her grave. When the funeral was over, the old man and his two sons returned to the homestead. They sat themselves down on the front porch and for a long time they talked and talked. They recalled a hundred and one stories about their mother. Some of those stories were humorous, and all of them were touching. Late in the evening the old man asked, "Where is Momma now? What's she doing right now? What is it like for her up there in heaven?" My friend and his brother, both of them brilliant theologians, began to speculate on what life after death was like. They tried to imagine what their mother might be doing at that very moment. They did their best to explain what the Scriptures had to say about heaven and the afterlife. They had beautiful things to tell their father, who hung anxiously on every word and description. When, having exhausted what their minds could imagine, his two sons had finished, the old man said, "Take me back. Take me back to that cemetery."

"We can't go back there now," my friend told his father. "It's after eleven o'clock. We'll go in the morning."

"Don't argue with me," the old man shot back. "Don't argue with a man who's just buried his wife of fifty-five years."

So they didn't argue with him; they took him back to the cemetery. With a flashlight the old man checked out his wife's grave. He made sure the flowers were arranged just the way she wanted them. He ran his fingers over the inscription on the tombstone. Then he stood back from the grave and said, "It's been a good fifty-five years, and, what's more, it ended just the way I wanted it to end. Boys, I'm happy that she died first."

I think that I know what he meant by that. When two people have a lifetime together in a common commitment to Christ, when they love each other with *philos*, when they share common goals and purposes, they each want the other to be the one to die first. Each wants the other to be delivered from the pain and the agony of burying his or her partner. Each wants the other to be delivered from the loneliness that comes from being left behind. It is easy to understand why the old man said, "It ended just the way I wanted it to end; she died first."

Then the old man stood back from the grave and put an arm around each of his two sons. He pulled them to him and he said, "We can go home now; we can go home. It's been a good day." My cynical friends fell silent. They were visibly moved by the story. I took advantage of their silence and said, "You and your romanticism could not possibly understand what was going on between those two people for fifty-five years. You even might have judged their relationship devoid of your expectations of eroticism. But I have a sneaking suspicion that those two old people had a depth in their relationship that makes your romanticism superficial by comparison."

I knew I had them. The argument was over. They had gained a glimpse of *philos,* the kind of love that grows between people who share the same goals and purposes in life, the kind of love between persons who have a common commitment to Jesus. And they recognized that it was superior to *eros.*

Our Lord invites each of us to experience this kind of relationship, one that makes the romance so bally-hooed by our society seem shallow by comparison. *Philos!* Why would anybody settle for romance when there is the possibility of experiencing *philos?*

Agapē is the third kind of love that the Greeks describe for us. *Agapē* love is so unique and overpower-

61

ing that it is hard to define. Perhaps only those who have fully surrendered to God can grasp the significance of *agapē* love. It is a love that God Himself generates in the lives of His people. When you surrender to God and pray that the Holy Spirit will invade your life, you will begin to experience this third kind of love. When God takes possession of your personhood, when His Spirit enters into your psyche, there will be created in you a love that those who resist God cannot possibly know. When you surrender to the Spirit of God, *agapē* is experienced with all of its power and glory.

Agapē is value-creating love. The object of love is made precious by *agapē*. *Agapē* does not consider whether or not the person being loved is attractive or worthy of love. Instead, the person becomes attractive and worthy because of being loved. To put it in simple language, if I love you because you are precious and beautiful, that is *eros*. But if you are precious and beautiful because I love you, that is *agapē*.

It is my firm belief that God expresses Himself uniquely in each and every human being. I am convinced that each person is a special revelation of God. Consequently, my relationship with my wife is conditioned by that fact. I find God revealed in her in a way that is unique. There is no other person in time and history who can reveal God to me in the special way in which He is revealed in her. She is like no other, because no other can give God to me as she does. Thus, my wife is infinitely unique to me and her uniqueness enables her to love me, and enables me to love her, in ways that would be impossible if I were married to any other person.

62

When my son, Bart, was a little boy, he had a favorite blanket. Many very young children become attached to their blankets. Bart's was so loved that he had a difficult time going to sleep without the feel of that blanket against his face. He established what Martin Buber would call an "I-Thou" relationship with his blanket. It even had a name—Gog. If it was misplaced, he was distraught. When it was lost, he was desperate. When it was in the wash, he would cry for it. We resolved that latter problem by tearing the blanket in half and giving him one half when the other was in the wash.

One night our family was traveling home from a speaking engagement and Bart was in the back seat. He was tired and consequently irritable. He started the whining that is so characteristic of exhausted children. I said to my wife, "Give him Gog." My wife responded, "I don't have it; don't you have it? The last thing I said to you when we left the house was, 'Pick up Gog!' "

But this was no time for my wife and me to argue. This was the time for unification against the common enemy sitting in the back seat. We knew we were in for an hour of obnoxious behavior. At that point I gladly would have given fifty dollars to anyone who could have immediately produced Gog, so that I could have silenced my son.

Looking at Gog, you would see no intrinsic value in the thing. As a matter of fact, when company came we always tried to hide it. Because the blanket had deteriorated into an old rag, objectively speaking, Gog had no value whatsoever. Nevertheless, Gog had fantastic value for us, value that Bart had created. His

63

attachment to the blanket had made it precious, not only to him, but to those of us who loved him. That's something like *agapē* love. The object of love may have no value. But value is created by virtue of the fact that the object is loved. *Agapē* love is unconditional. It does not have to be earned. It is given even when it is not deserved, and that is the way that God loves us and the way that we are supposed to love each other.

A brilliant example of *agapē* love has been set forth by Lorraine Hansberry in her powerful play, *A Raisin in the Sun.* The play is about a black family that lives in Chicago's Southside. The father of the household dies, leaving a small legacy as a result of an insurance policy. I believe the family inherits about ten thousand dollars. The mother wants to use the money as a means to fulfill one of her fondest dreams. She imagines herself moving her family into a little house on the other side of town. She dreams of a bungalow complete with shutters and window boxes filled with flowers. Those window boxes filled with flowers had come to symbolize the bliss that she believed such a house would bring to her and her family.

The problem is that her son wants the money in order to go into business. This young man has never had a chance. He has never had a break, and never had a job. Now he has a friend who has a "deal." This friend convinces the son that with his deal, they could start a business together that would make them all kinds of money. Then the son could do good things for his family. He had always wanted to do good things for his family.

Pathetically, he begs and pleads for the money. At

first his mother refuses to give it to him, but eventually she knows that she must give in. How can she deny her son, who has never had a chance to do anything worthwhile with his life? How can she turn her back on his pleading for a chance to do something for the family? She puts over half the money in his hands, and you can imagine what happens next.

The family is gathered together at home when another victim of the swindler drops in and reveals the news that the son's "friend" has taken the money and skipped town. Head bowed and shoulders slumped, the son confesses the whole story. His sister, Beneatha, wastes no time tearing into him verbally. She rips him up and down. She pours out her contempt for him. She condemns him for having been so stupid. She screams at him for having lost, for them all, the only escape route from the hell in which they have lived for years. When she finishes her tirade, the mother speaks, "I thought I taught you to love him."

Beneatha shouts back, "Love him? There is nothing left to love."

Then the mother says, "There is always something left to love. And if you ain't learned that, you ain't learned nothing. Have you cried for that boy today? I don't mean for yourself and for the family 'cause we lost the money. I mean for him; what he been through and what it done to him. Child, when do you think is the time to love somebody the most; when they done good and made things easy for everybody? Well then, you ain't through learning—because that ain't the time at all. It's when he's at his lowest and can't believe in hisself 'cause the world done whipped

65

him so. When you starts measuring somebody, measure him right, child, measure him right. Make sure you done take into account what hills and valleys he come through before he got to wherever he is."

That's *agapē* love. That's the love that flows even when it's not deserved. That mother in the play shows us something of God's love.

God loves you when you have done well. He's pleased when you've accomplished something worthwhile. But the good news is that He loves you even when you haven't done well. He loves you even when you mess up. He loves you when you've done terrible things. He loves you even when you've done the most despicable things imaginable. In spite of anything you might have done, God still loves you. In spite of what you are, God still loves you. That's what *agapē* is all about. *Agapē* love, unlike *eros*, is exceedingly stable. It is a never-ending love that never wavers or, to use the words of the Apostle Paul in 1 Corinthians 13, "Love never faileth." What is equally significant is that this *agapē* love of God can flow through one person into the lives of others. Each of us is capable of becoming a conduit through which God's love is "shed abroad" for others to experience.

This fact has significantly affected my relationship with my wife. As I mentioned earlier, I was romantically "turned on" shortly after I met her. *Eros* carried me into my marriage. However, *eros* would not have been sufficient to maintain marriage. It has been *agapē* that has done that. God loving my wife through me is what has held me close to her over the years. Like most other people, I've been aware of possible erotic "turn-ons" to other women I meet. But the *agapē* love of God keeps me faithful to my wife.

Imagine me starting my day at work. I get to my office. I get out my research material and spread it over my desk. Then my research assistant, vivacious and shapely Jane, comes in. Her spike heels click on the tile floor as she hurries over to my desk. "Good morning, Dr. Campolo," she beams. "Is there *anything* I can do for you this morning?"

I don't know how to answer that one. I know; I shock you with the mere suggestion of what could start flashing through my mind. You say, "You're supposed to be a Christian! You're supposed to be a man of God!"

Of course I'm a Christian and I try to be a man of God. But Christians experience the same turn-ons and temptations as everybody else. The difference for Christians is that they can call upon the Lord and ask for the inner strength to overcome these temptations. As Jane leans over my desk, I mumble to myself, "God, your property is in danger."

When romantic turn-ons tempt me, there is always the constant *agapē* love of God that keeps me faithful to my wife. Furthermore, God sensitizes me to the fact that he not only dwells in me, but in my wife also. To be unfaithful to her would mean that I would be unfaithful to Him. To hurt her would mean that I would hurt Him. The love of God flowing through me to my wife, along with the presence of God that I discern in my wife, is all that I've got in the end to keep me faithful. I will be forever grateful for this *agapē* love from God because it alone is what I find to be capable of overpowering the romantic temptations generated by *eros*. Even in my everyday relationship with my wife, I can verify the truth of that old communion hymn:

67

IT'S FRIDAY,
BUT SUNDAY'S COMIN'

> Blest be the tie that binds
> Our hearts in Christian love;
> The fellowship of Christian minds
> Is like to that above.*

Before we leave this discussion of love, I want to make one more assertion. I stated earlier that romance dies shortly after marriage. I had better correct that to read that romance dies *unless* it is resurrected and revitalized under the influence of deeper kinds of love. I have found that *philos* and *agapē* so condition my relationship with my wife that romance is constantly breaking loose between us. I find myself falling in love with my wife over and over again. All the bubbling excitement, eroticism and ecstasy that characterizes teenage romance is experienced at my ripe old age of forty-eight.

There is a poem that was given to me by a friend when I was fourteen years old. I have never forgotten it. It reminds me that romance can always be rekindled if there are spiritual dimensions to one's personality. It goes:

> Walk soft where once love grew
> For every spring is proof of resurrection
> And every Christmas is evidence
> Of the rebirth of love.

68

In his film *The Four Seasons*, Alan Alda is asked whether or not he still gets romantic about his wife. He answers, "It comes in waves." I would have to

---

* "Blest Be the Tie That Binds," John Fawcett, 1782.

say the same thing. Romance comes in waves for me too. I don't always feel it. I don't think that most people *always* feel it. But I do feel it. It still overtakes me with all of its wonder and bliss. It still gives me fits. It still adds a delicious dimension to my life. What is more, it happens with increasing frequency as the years go by. You've got to admit—that's good news.

To those who are looking for the kind of love that makes for joy and for fulfillment in life, I am not ashamed to recommend the kind of love experiences that flow out of a relationship with Jesus. *I am not ashamed of the Gospel of Christ,* because it has met my need for love.

CHAPTER FIVE

Jesus Meets
Our Need
for the
Miraculous

When I say that Jesus meets our need for the miraculous, I am usually greeted by a sophisticated skepticism from people who claim that those who need miraculous things to happen in their lives belong to another era. These skeptics who want to assign me to the Middle Ages suggest that I would fit in better with medieval monks than with people in our modern scientific world. However, even these pseudosophisticates have a need for the miraculous. They may not recognize it—that need may be unconscious—but sooner or later it will surface. It always does. The citizens of this souped-up, jet-propelled, neon-lighted, computerized society still have a craving for wonder and awe. They may conceal that need beneath a veneer of rational positivism, but emotionally the hunger for the supernatural still burns within them. How else can we find explanations for such incongruities in our world as the sections on the occult on book shelves in Ivy League universities, and movies on the supernatural that draw overflowing crowds (e.g., *Poltergeist, The Exorcist* and *The Omen*).

Fyodor Dostoyevsky, the Russian novelist who many say has given us the most brilliant descriptions of the human psyche in modern times, clearly saw the

73

need people have for the miraculous to invade their mundane lives. In a section of his novel *The Brothers Karamazov* which he names "The Grand Inquisitor," he points out that human beings cannot live without the expectation of the miraculous. He says:

> Man seeks not so much God as the miraculous. And as man cannot bear to be without the miraculous, he will create new miracles of his own for himself, and will worship deeds of sorcery and witchcraft, though he might be a hundred times over a rebel, heretic and infidel.

We are not quite the rational creatures that we think we are. In times of crisis we cry out for miracles. When a tragedy like cancer befalls us, we long for supernatural cures. When life gets out of control, we crave divine intervention.

So many contemporary theologians seem to be embarrassed by the miraculous. They appear determined to express religion in totally rational terms. They exclude talk of miracles from their discussions and reduce "god talk" to logical and philosophical systems. That is probably why most people aren't interested in modern theology; it's all so categorical, it's all so intellectual. It fails to grasp that a great deal of Christianity transcends the intellectual and that there are dimensions to our faith that just won't fit into rational boxes.

74

Several years ago, I was invited to be a guest lecturer at a small college in the Midwest. It was one of those schools that had been founded by religious people but had lost its religious mooring. While the school had become secularized, there were a few remaining signs of its previous religious affiliation. One of them was an annual religious emphasis week. Most religious colleges have such weeks in which an effort is made to religiously "psych up" the student body. Usually these efforts produce little change. This particular college thought I could do the job for them and brought me in to resurrect their dead. My assignment was to interest an apathetic student body that was forced to attend my lectures about how Christianity was supposedly exciting and intellectually tenable.

The college had scheduled the lectures for evenings. At the end of my presentation on the second night a woman came down the aisle of the auditorium carrying her child in her arms. The child was crippled and in braces, and the woman was obviously not a member of the student body. Furthermore, she had a strange look in her eyes.

"What do you want?" I asked.

She answered, "God told me to come."

I didn't know how to handle that. It seemed to me that if God had told her to come, the least He could have done was to tell me that she was coming.

I asked, "Well, is there something you think I can do for you?"

She said, "You are supposed to heal my child."

I responded, "Dear lady, I don't have the gift of healing. There are a variety of gifts according to the Bible. Some people are given the gift of tongues, some the gift of prophesy, some the gift of healing and some the gift of teaching. Teaching is my gift."

I had a strong inclination to simply point to my bald head and say, "If I could heal, would I look

75

like this?" I told her that healing just was not my thing, but she wouldn't back off. "God told me to come," she said even more emphatically.

The students quickly picked up what was happening, and I could hear whispers and titters of laughter spreading over the audience. There was no question that they were delighted to see my discomfort. The chaplain of the college recognized that I was in an embarrassing situation. He was a very typical college chaplain. I'm sure you know the type. They wear turtleneck sweaters, and chains with big crosses around their necks. They smoke pipes and they try to look very relevant. He came over to us and he asked, "What's the problem, Doctor?"

I said, "This lady wants me to heal her kid."

He asked, "Do you want some help?"

"Please!" I shot back.

The chaplain spoke to the audience and said, "Those who do not believe that this child is going to be healed this evening, please leave the auditorium. If you are not absolutely convinced that this child will have his legs straightened through prayer, I want you to get out of here. Not even Jesus could perform miracles or mighty works when He was surrounded by people who were filled with unbelief."

"Hey," I thought to myself, "that's not bad for a theologically liberal college chaplain. That's really a smart move."

It was a smart move, because once he said that, almost everyone in the auditorium got up and left. With one statement he had cleared the place. All that were left were five Pentecostal kids, and they were already into their thing, lifting hands into the air and praying in tongues. I figured the guy had gotten me off the hook, that I was safe and clear.

I asked, "What do we do now?"

He answered, "We're taking the kid out back into the kitchen."

"What are you going to do in the kitchen?" was my response.

He said, "We're going to anoint the child's head with oil."

"Oil? What kind of oil?" I asked.

"Del Monte!" he answered with a smile on his face.

Somehow that answer lacked the kind of spirituality that I was expecting. I thought he might have something like holy water from Israel or some special ointment that had been blessed by the pope.

I asked, "Are you kidding?"

He said, "Look, Campolo; it says in the Book of James that if somebody needs healing, the elders of the church are to anoint the person's head with oil, lay hands on him, and pray for healing. So, unless you have a better idea, you had better do what the Book tells you."

Now that is not bad advice, no matter what the source. So we went into the back room and did what we were supposed to do. We followed the instructions in the Book of James like it was a cookbook. First we applied the oil, then we laid on our hands, and then we prayed. I had invited the five Pentecostal kids to join us, so they had their hands on the kid's head too. I figured that if anybody had anything going for him, I wanted him in on this.

I started to pray. It was one of those phony prayers that are all too common when we pray in the presence

77

of others. I think you know what I mean. So often when others are present, we have a tendency to utter pat religious phrases that are high-sounding and that communicate an image of spirituality rather than concentrating on God. I can still hear myself praying: "O God, the great Creator of the Universe; O thou who in the days of old has healed the blind, made the lame to walk and raised up the dead, we beseech Thee in this hour to be present and among us—" And I stopped dead. In the midst of my prayer my Pentecostal friends stopped their praying in tongues. We all felt it. We all felt a strange and awesome presence break loose in our midst. Unexpectedly, the Holy Spirit was among us. The Holy Spirit had descended into our midst. His Presence was overpowering and disturbing and shattered my pretended religiosity. The experience must have been something similar to what Isaiah described in the sixth chapter of his book. There he said:

> In the year that King Uzziah died I saw the Lord sitting upon a throne, high and lifted up; and his train filled the temple. Above him stood the seraphim; each had six wings: with two he covered his face, and with two he covered his feet, and with two he flew. And one called to another and said: "Holy, holy, holy is the Lord of hosts; the whole earth is full of his glory." And the foundations of the thresholds shook at the voice of him who called, and the house was filled with smoke. And I said: "Woe is me! For I am lost; for I am a man of unclean lips, and I dwell in the midst of a people of unclean lips; for my eyes have seen the King, the Lord of hosts!"
>
> *Isaiah 6:1–5,* RSV

78

It is an awesome thing to stand in the presence of the Almighty. I didn't know how to react. Instinctively, I removed my hand and I felt terribly ashamed. My Pentecostal friends withdrew their hands too. I must admit that I fully expected that the child would be healed. The power of the Spirit was so overwhelming that a miraculous healing would not have surprised me. But the child was not healed. After some awkward excuses and explanations we all got out of the room and I quickly left the building. The rest of the lectures in the series unfolded in a very uneventful way. I was glad when the week was over and I could get back to my home, away from that strange and mysterious situation.

Three years after that I was a guest speaker in a church in St. Louis. When the worship service was over a lady came up to me and asked, "Do you remember who I am?"

"Yes!" I answered. "It was three years ago that I met you. You brought your little boy for healing. We prayed for him. How is your little boy?"

She said, "I came here today because I wanted you to see him. Here he is."

There beside her, with no braces on his legs, her little boy was standing as straight and as whole as any boy could be. His legs weren't twisted anymore.

"How did this happen?" I asked.

She answered, "We prayed! Don't you remember? We prayed! The next morning he woke up crying. I noticed that his braces were a little tight. I loosened them and his legs straightened just a little. It happened again the next morning, and then it happened

79

again and again and again. It kept happening until his legs were made straight."

I didn't know how to handle any of that. The situation was beyond me.

A few days later I was back in my hometown, Philadelphia, having lunch with two academic colleagues. One was a professor of religion from the University of Pennsylvania. I explained to my friends what had happened, and one of them said, "Well, Tony, I have to be honest with you. My theology does not allow for that sort of thing to happen." Isn't that wild? I mean, you've got to smile at that response. *His* theology did not allow for that to happen!

I said, "Charlie, I don't want to upset you, but maybe—just maybe—God is greater than your theology. Maybe—just maybe—God is able to do abundantly more than your theology could ever hope or think."

I think that a problem with a lot of theologians is that they've got God in a little box. They are quick to tell you what God can do and what He can't do. They write books on God and in a couple of hundred pages they attempt to tell you everything that can be told about the Almighty. Someday I would like to tell all the rationalistic theologians in the world that God transcends their categorical terms. He breaks out of their *a priori* assumptions about Him. God cannot be put into their theological constructs any more than you can put new wine in old wineskins. The new wine will expand and tear up the old wineskins. Likewise, God breaks out of any theological system that we try to construct in our attempt to box Him in.

I want to make it very clear that I do not understand

the miraculous. I don't understand miracles. I don't understand healing. And I don't understand why some people, some deeply godly people, pray for healing and do not experience it. I don't understand why God doesn't intercede and heal whenever His people pray in faith. And I know so many examples which demonstrate that godly people who believe in the power of prayer and implore God for healing do not have their requests met. On the other hand, it sometimes seems that others who are far less deserving experience the therapeutic power of the Almighty.

I can't figure out the ways of God. After all, there is no human who can. Isaiah 55:8 says that His ways are not our ways and His thoughts are not our thoughts. I react vehemently to those popular preachers who communicate via TV and radio to millions of Americans that God will heal any person who asks, using the right formula. I believe that they are responsible for stimulating expectations that may not be fulfilled. Those who claim that God will heal every person who prays in faith, believing, create heartbreak and disillusionment among more people than can be imagined.

I know of one case in which a family was given the news that the father was seriously ill with cancer and in all probability would be dead in a matter of months. This man's children were very close to him. They loved him deeply and the news of his impending death shattered them emotionally. One sister, responding to the claims of a famous television preacher, wrote a letter to that preacher and asked what was necessary for their father to be healed. The evangelist responded (probably with one of those let-

81

ters done by a computer word processor) that if everyone in the family would confess the sin in his or her life and, as purified believers, pray for healing, then healing would come for their father.

To the best of their ability each of the family members did as they were instructed. They confessed their sins. They asked the Holy Spirit to purify their hearts and they prayed with intensity that their father would be healed. The sad news was that their father was not healed. He died.

After the father's death the daughter once again wrote to the evangelist. The response that came was most despicable. The evangelist said in his letter that the reason their father had not been healed was that there was still some sin in the life of one of the family members. That sent several of these young people into the depths of sadness. Each of them went on a guilt trip, thinking that it might have been something in his or her life that was responsible for the father's death. Each of them went through a long process of self-accusation. I doubt if any of them will ever overcome the effects of that letter.

To theology like that of the TV evangelist letter-writer, I say, "Hogwash!" I believe in the miraculous, but I do not believe that anybody can control the miraculous. Some contemporary evangelists are more like magicians who claim to possess personal power than servants of God who do as the Bible commands and leave to the discretion of the Almighty those who are to be healed and those who are not to be healed.

It is my strong belief that healings and miracles are not the normative thing in the life of the church,

82

but rather that they are "signs" of the Kingdom of God. I believe that through them God is pointing to what will happen to all of the sick and the maimed in the life beyond the grave. Healings are unusual occurrences that tell every person who is physically disabled or sickly that one day, someday, he will be whole and well. Healings are declaration of the news that the time will come when each of us will have a new body, complete, healthy and free from the possibility of decay. But promising that each person who prays will be healed here on earth is a very wrong thing to do.

Many of us know of Joni Eareckson Tada. This beautiful young woman who is paralyzed has prayed and prayed and has had prayers said for her, but she will honestly admit that she does not think that healing is for her. An exceptional woman, she has been one of the most brilliant testimonies for Christ in our time. Her life has become an example for many handicapped people, demonstrating that they can lead lives that are productive, effective and a blessing to others even though their bodies do not function as they would like them to. To say that Joni Eareckson Tada is somehow lacking in faith or hasn't prayed properly seems obscene.

I believe in the miraculous. I thrive on the awe and the wonder that it generates. I know the truth set forth by Dostoyevsky that we have a need for the miraculous so that we do not become smothered by the routinized expectations of a mundane world. We need the miraculous because we need to believe that this world of scientific predictability can be tran-

83

scended. The miraculous is what gives us a basis for hope even when the circumstances of life tell us that there is no room for hope.

I am not ashamed of the Gospel of Christ, because it meets my need for the miraculous. And I am sure it will meet your need for the miraculous.

CHAPTER SIX

Jesus Meets
Our Need
for a
Purpose in Life

Viktor Frankl, the Viennese psychotherapist, once said that the basic need for human beings is to have a purpose and meaning for life. According to Frankl, life is intolerable for people who lack purpose. He discovered this truth while imprisoned in a Nazi concentration camp. During the years he spent there, he utilized his time studying differences between people who were able to survive the horrors of prison camp and those who were destroyed by them. After careful scrutiny and analysis of his fellow prisoners, he reached a clear conclusion: those who could survive the prison camp were those who had clearly defined goals for living, while those who lacked a clear purpose for life quickly capitulated to the subhuman conditions created by the Nazis and died.

The fact that every human being needs a purpose for living can provide an important basis for evangelism. Some of my friends work with the Campus Crusade for Christ movement. They have been able to appeal to college and university students and get them to accept Christ as Savior and Lord by making it clear to them that through a commitment to Christ, they can come into a meaningful existence and a glorious reason for living. These Campus Crusade evangelists often utilize a little booklet entitled *The Four Spiritual Laws.* The first of these laws is: "God has a wonderful plan for your life." That simple statement has had fantastic appeal for college and university students who have intelligence, much knowledge, and numerous opportunities in life, but lack a plan for living. The great truth expressed in the first of the four spiritual laws is Good News to them, and they often give their lives to Christ because of the promise that a life in Christ has purpose.

I think that it is essential for every human being to know that his or her existence is not simply a biological accident but has been willed by God. I believe that it is of ultimate importance for every person to know that God is inviting him or her into a relationship in which a purpose and a plan can be worked out and delineated. God wants each of us to discover, in dialogue with Him, that there can be a meaningful plan for life.

It is important to affirm that there is something great that you will never do unless you come to Jesus. There is something wonderful that God will never be able to accomplish through you until you surrender to His will. There is something of ultimate importance that God wants you to achieve for Him. I am convinced that God has a special mission for you to perform in His name. When you come to grips with Jesus, you will come to know that purpose. When you discern His mission for you, you will know what your life is all about. Then, and only then, will your quest for meaning and purpose be realized.

When Jesus died on the cross and saved you from sin, he did so not only to get you into heaven, but

for an even more important reason—as strange as
that statement may seem. Jesus saved you through
His death on Calvary's tree in order to make you
into a person who could do magnificent things for
others in His name. He saved you so that He could
work through you and accomplish things that He
wants to have done in this world. Jesus wants to eliminate hunger, and He saved you in order that He might
eliminate the hunger of many people through you.
Jesus wants to clothe the naked, and He saved you
in order that He might be able to clothe them through
your efforts. Jesus wants to deliver the oppressed into
freedom and bring justice to the downtrodden, and
He wants you to be one of the instruments through
which such important things can be done. Jesus saved
you in order that you might be an agent for His revolution in the world. He saved you so that through you
He might bring about some of the changes that are
essential if He is to make this world into the kind
of world that He willed for it to be when He created
it.

I did not always understand this important truth.
In my early days as a Christian, I thought that the
primary reason that Jesus saved me was in order that
I could go to heaven when I died. In those days I
thought that everything worthwhile was waiting for
me in the life after death, and that what was going
on in this world wasn't really important.

I want to affirm at this point that I do believe in
heaven and that I am absolutely convinced that those
who believe in Jesus go there when this life is ended.
However, I have, of late, become convinced that our
Lord was more concerned about getting us to live

89

life in this world in a meaningful way than He was about getting us into heaven after death. He told His disciples that He had come that they might have life and that they might have it more abundantly. This fact is emphatically communicated to us through Scripture. Furthermore, He wants us to learn that this life can be had *only* through loving service to others in His name. His message is that joy, aliveness and fulfillment can be had only in giving our lives to the work that He has for us to do. It is not in getting what *we* want, but in doing what *He* wants that we become self-actualized persons with a sense of ecstasy about life. Every person needs something of ultimate importance to do with his or her life, and the Good News is that Jesus has something special for each one of us to do.

I am amazed at how many people do not recognize that serving others for Jesus is the only proper response that anyone can give to God for the great things that He has done for us. Such people fail to see that there is no way to be "holy" other than by being an instrument set apart by God to fulfill His purposes in our world. In reality, the word "holy" has been found by etymologists to mean "set apart." Thus, holiness is not a "better-than-you" piety, but a willingness to let God set you apart for His work. Unfortunately, too many people think that the way to express the lordship of Christ in their lives is by acting piously superior to others, when in reality it means becoming the servants of others.

My purpose here is not to condemn piety. (Some of my best friends are pious.) But sometimes it does make me a bit uneasy. When I was a new convert, my Christian friends communicated to me that pious was what I was supposed to be. They told me that if I were going to be a true Christian, then I had to live according to a list of rules which they said would set me apart from the world. In most of the sermons that I heard, I was urged to follow these rules more than I was urged to become a servant to others. It seemed as though there were a thousand and one messages from the pulpit suggesting that the Christian life was set in negatives rather than positives. I was told about a host of things that Christians were not supposed to do, but I did not get a very clear image of what Christians were supposed to do for others. Members of our church youth group would jokingly chant,

> We don't smoke
> or dance or chew
> and we don't go
> with girls who do.

Being a Christian was essentially defined as the giving up of "worldly pleasures" rather than as a call to commitment to the work that God has for us to do in this world.

I can still remember one preacher pounding the pulpit and shouting, "Dancing stimulates the lust of the flesh!" He went on to describe in lascivious detail the ways that dancing pumped up the hormones and stimulated sexual cravings. By the time he finished he had me fantasizing and saying to myself, "Wow! That sounds like fun."

I don't want to provide too much of a put-down

91

of those sermons about dancing, because in many respects that preacher was right. I realize this whenever I happen to catch some of the modern dancing on television. Even a casual glance at most of that dancing will make it fairly obvious that the pelvic movements of those go-go types have the capacity to excite all kinds of sensual desires. You may be inclined to call me "a dirty old man," but it seems to me that if two young people stand in front of each other erotically vibrating for hours at a time, they are going to end up very sexually "turned on." If they are *not* turned on by those gyrations, I'm not as ready to call them "spiritual" as I am to call them "dead." However, there may be some hypocrisy on the part of the churches that condemn dancing. Too often these same churches that preach against dancing are the ones that sponsor church hayrides. I don't want to seem cynical, but I've been on church hayrides, and often what takes place in the straw makes what goes on on the dance floor seem mild by comparison.

Another mark of piety that was big during my teenage years was staying away from the movies. I heard evangelists shout at audiences, "What if you're in the movie house when the trumpet sounds and the Lord returns? What if Jesus returns to earth and finds *you* in the movies?"

92 Every time I went to the movies I was scared to death. I was sure that I was going to get halfway through the picture and the trumpet would sound and the Lord would return. But worst of all, I think that what worried me most was that I wouldn't get to see the end of the movie.

Smoking was another "no-no" among people with whom I ran in my early Christian days. And I must admit that I still have all kinds of negative reactions to smoking. I think it's a terrible habit. As far as I'm concerned, the family that smokes together chokes together. As a teenager, I always felt that kissing a girl that smoked would be like licking an ashtray.

Did you ever get on an airplane and sit in the non-smoking section only to find that the guy next to you lights up a cigarette and lets the smoke drift right into your face? While you're choking, he usually says, "You don't mind if I smoke, do you?" I almost feel like responding, "Not if you don't mind if I vomit."

If I seem only to be mocking the mentality that condemns smoking, dancing and drinking, I am failing to make my point. I think that these practices, along with many others, can raise some very serious questions for those who want to establish a Christian lifestyle. However, I become upset whenever Christians make the abandoning of such practices the essence of the Christian faith. I react against those who would make this kind of personal piety the essence of Christianity. The truth is that you can give up smoking, dancing and the movies and be nowhere near what is important to a Christian lifestyle.

In the days of Jesus, the Pharisees, who lived according to the letter of the law, were always trying to outdo themselves in measuring up to the requisites of the piety that had emerged in the Jewish society. When Jesus negatively reacted to their lifestyle, He made it clear that the essence of godliness was not to be achieved in a legalistic lifestyle of personal piety, but in loving sacrifice to poor people and in service

93

to the lost. Jesus made it clear that it is possible to be very pious and yet miss the real meaning of godliness.

It is about time that we take seriously the claim that Jesus made when He said that if any man would be His disciple, he would have to deny himself, sell what he has, pick up the cross and follow Him. The willingness to sacrifice everything that we are and have in order to serve Christ and the people that He has called us to love is the only acceptable response to what Jesus has done for us on Calvary. Personal piety is no substitute for loving sacrifice.

> I urge you therefore, brethren, by the mercies of God, to present your bodies a living and holy sacrifice, acceptable to God, which is your spiritual service of worship, and do not be conformed to this world, but be transformed by the renewing of your mind, that you may prove what the will of God is, that which is good and acceptable and perfect.
>
> *Romans 12:1–2*, NASB

Most of us have been kidding ourselves. We've been trying to pretend that we can live lives of typical middle-class affluence in a world with people who are experiencing desperate poverty, and still call ourselves Christians. We try to avoid passages like 1 John 3:17–18, which tells us, "But whoever has the world's goods, and beholds his brother in need and closes his heart against him, how does the love of God abide in him? Little children, let us not love with word or with tongue, but in deed and truth" (NASB). Those verses raise crucial questions: How can any person say that he loves Jesus and not respond to the suffer-

94

ings of the people that Jesus loves? How is it possible
for anyone to say that he or she is imitating Jesus
while holding onto surplus wealth in the face of those
who are craving food for survival? Does not being a
Christian mean feeding the hungry, clothing the
naked, freeing the captives, ministering to the sick?
Are not such actions infinitely more important than
adhering to the rituals of personal piety that have
been created by religious legalists?

I head up a small missionary organization called
the Evangelical Association for the Promotion of Education which has developed a number of projects in
Third World countries. One of these projects is an
orphanage designed to care for children who have
been abandoned by their parents and are victims of
extreme malnutrition. These are children who are so
debilitated and run down that unless they receive intensive treatment they will die within a few months.
We planned for this orphanage to care for fifty such
children, in the belief that an orphanage of that size
would take care of all such children living in the urban
slum that our organization had targeted to help. The
day that we opened the orphanage, we took a bus
and drove it to the slum region where these desperate
children lived. However, instead of fifty children waiting for us we found four times that many. All of them
were in the same debilitated and sickly condition. All
of them seemed to be so malnourished that death,
for them, lurked in the immediate future. We could
care for only fifty of them, which meant that most
of them would be denied the loving care they needed
to survive. Over the next few hours we had to go
through the incredibly cruel process of selecting
which of those children would live and which would

95

die. We had to decide which children would come to live in our orphanage and which would continue to live in the slums until death overtook them.

There is no way that you can imagine the pain of that process and the emotional turmoil that accompanied the choices and decision making. But we did what we had to do, and when we completed the agonizing task, we loaded the chosen children on the bus and sent them off to the orphanage. The priest who served the Catholic church in that slum expressed his gratitude to us for doing what we could and shared our distress over having to turn away so many needy children. Then he asked the children who had been left behind to sing a song for us to show their appreciation for our having helped the others. I felt my insides twisted and torn as I listened to these children with their stomachs elongated because of malnutrition, standing on legs that were so emaciated that I wondered how they could support the weight of their bodies. I could hardly listen as they sang for us, in their native language, the familiar gospel chorus

> God is so good,
> God is so good,
> God is so good,
> He's so good to me.

96   I didn't want to hear it. But they kept on singing,

> He loves me so,
> He loves me so,
> He loves me so,
> He's so good to me.

Something within me seemed to cry out in protest. Gritting my teeth, I said to myself, "It's not true! God isn't good to them. He doesn't love them or else He would not leave them in this condition. He would do something if He loved them. He would deliver them from this hunger. He would cure their sicknesses." Then it dawned on me. God *did* love them. He did have a plan to deliver them from hunger and sickness. That plan was to bring them love and help through people like you and me. His plan was to reach out to these children through those who are willing to sacrifice their lives to help them in the name of Christ. They were suffering, not because God didn't care, but because people like us think that we can be religious without responding to the needs of such suffering children. If all of the people who express their religiosity with egocentric piety would change and express their commitment to Christ by giving their wealth, and even their lives, in service to suffering people, such children would not have to be turned away to pain and death.

There is a tendency for many people in our "rational" society to make Christianity into a commitment to abstract principles, rather than making it into a commitment to others. I can remember, as a boy, going through the catechism class in which I was taught that "the chief end of man is to love God and to serve Him forever." That statement is beautiful, but very often we fail to understand *how* God is served. There is a tendency for us to make loving God into nothing more than a private, inward meditative trip. Meditation is important. I would be the last one to argue with the fact that God invites us to encounter

97

Him through inwardness and meditation. But our Christian faith must move beyond meditation. I believe that it is crucial for us to acknowledge that the Jesus whom we find within ourselves is, first of all, the Jesus who confronts us in the form of a neighbor who is in need. It is essential for us to recognize that the God we can come to know in mystical contemplation chooses to incarnate Himself in the last and in the least of the hurting people who confront us day by day. I am absolutely convinced that before we can meditate on Him and contemplate His wonder, we must first encounter Him in those persons who confront us in need. In them He waits to be discovered. In them He waits to be encountered. In them He waits to be loved. It is through them that we learn of Him.

Some years ago I was doing missionary work in Haiti and in the Dominican Republic. One afternoon, near the border separating those two countries, I stood on the edge of a grass landing strip waiting for a small Piper Cub airplane to come to pick me up and fly me back to the capital city. As I stood there, a woman came toward me. In her hands she was holding her baby. The child's stomach was swelled to four or five times normal size because of malnutrition. The arms and legs of the little boy were so spindly that they appeared to be nothing more than bones covered with skin. He was a black child but his hair had taken on the rust color that evidences a lack of protein. The child's mouth was hanging open, and his eyes were rolled back so that they appeared to be white bulges in his skull. The baby was dirty and filthy and obviously close to death. The

woman held the child up to me and then began pleading for me to take her child. "Please, mister, please
take my baby; take my baby with you," she begged.
"Take my baby to your country. Feed my baby. Take
care of my baby. Don't let my baby die."

I didn't know what to do. I couldn't take her baby.
There were hundreds of babies like this in the surrounding countryside. What could I do in the face
of such overpowering suffering? I pushed her away
and I told her, "I can't help you. I can't take your
baby. Do you understand? There's nothing I can do!"

She pleaded again, "Mister, don't let my baby die.
Please, mister, don't let my baby die. Take my baby.
Please take my baby with you."

Again I pushed her aside but she kept on pleading
with me, "Take my baby. Don't let my baby die.
Please, mister, have mercy on my baby."

I was relieved when I saw the Piper Cub airplane
come into sight and touch down at the edge of the
grass landing strip. As it rolled toward me I ran out
to meet it. I wanted to get away from that woman
and her baby. But she came running after me. She
was screaming at the top of her lungs, "Take my baby!
Take my baby! Don't let my baby die!" She was hyster-
ical in her pleading as I climbed into the airplane
and closed the plexiglass door. Before the pilot could
turn the airplane around for the takeoff, she was
alongside us, banging the fuselage of the airplane and
screaming at me, "Don't let my baby die! Don't let
my baby die!"

The engine revved up. The pilot released the brakes
of the plane and we began to move away from the
woman and down the landing strip. She ran alongside

99

the plane, still clutching her horribly emaciated baby and screaming at me to take her child. At last the plane lifted into the air, and as we soared into the sky, the pilot banked so that we turned and flew back over the landing field. As we did so, I got one last look at that woman who by then was standing motionless in the middle of the landing strip clutching her baby. We flew away and I tried to put that woman and her baby out of my mind. But I couldn't. Halfway back to the capital it hit me. It dawned on me who that baby was. I realized who it was that I had left behind on that landing strip. The name of that child was Jesus. Regardless of the name his parents had given him at birth, I knew that his name was Jesus. It was Jesus who was incarnated in the feeble, sickly frame. It was Jesus who had been held out to me for love and care. It was Jesus whom I had shut out of my life.

One day, some day, the Lord is going to say to me, "I was hungry and you didn't feed me; I was naked and you didn't clothe me; I was sick and you didn't care for me; I was a stranger and you didn't take me in." The twenty-fifth chapter of Matthew assures me that the Lord is going to say that to me when I stand before His judgment seat. And when I ask, "When did I see you hungry and not feed you? When did I see you sick and not minister to you? When did I see you a stranger and not take you in?" He is going to say to me, "On that landing strip on the Haitian border. For inasmuch as you failed to do it unto the least of these little ones, you failed to do it unto me."

Too many of us think that being a Christian is sim-

100

ply a matter of believing the right stuff. Too many
of us think that if we give intellectual assent to the
right religious propositions, we will be part of the
Kingdom of God. We can easily delude ourselves into
assuming that simply having the right theology makes
us into God's children. Well, that's not true. The Epis-
tle of James tells us that even Satan believes all the
right stuff. If having an orthodox theology makes a
person a Christian, then Satan is the best Christian
of all. What is more, Satan trembles at the acknowl-
edgment of biblical truths. He believes everything that
an evangelical Christian ought to believe. Satan believes in the deity of Christ, the virgin birth, the miracles, the resurrection and the second coming. His
theology is orthodox to the core. He can quote Scripture at the snap of a finger. Nevertheless, he remains
estranged from God and the furthest removed from
God's Kingdom.

Being a Christian is much more than believing the
right stuff. Being a Christian is giving yourself, and
all that you have, to the One in whom you say you
believe. It's giving yourself, without reservation, to
the Jesus who incarnates Himself in the suffering children who are waiting for us to find Him in them and
love Him in them. Satan's theology may be all right,
but he doesn't love Jesus and he is not about to minister to the needs of those desperate people in whom
the living Jesus incarnates Himself in our time.

America has twenty million pet dogs, and I readily
admit that I have the nicest one of them all. But we
must be aware of the fact that of those twenty million
dogs, 73 percent are overweight. After we overcome
the giggles that result from imagining millions and

101

millions of fat dogs stumbling around in comfortable American homes, we have to ask some very serious questions about ourselves. What kind of people would overfeed pet animals while letting children in Haiti and Somalia and Ethiopia starve to death? These children *are* starving to death, you know. Five hundred million people go to bed every night suffering from hunger. Every night some ten thousand children die from malnutrition. And while all of this takes place, there is a high level of indifference among affluent Americans. We who would become upset if our pet dogs missed a meal ignore the agonies of those who have nothing to eat.

One evening I went to eat at a restaurant in Port-au-Prince, Haiti. I sat down at a table in the front of the restaurant, next to the window. I ordered my food and it was quickly served. Then, just as I was about to plunge the fork into the food, I looked to my right and discovered four little Haitian boys standing there on the other side of the window. With their noses pressed flat against the glass, they were staring at my food. They did not even seem to notice me. Instead, their eyes were riveted on the food on my plate. They were dirty, almost naked children—some of the hundreds who wander the streets of Port-au-Prince, belonging to no one, and for whom no one cares. They were the throw-away-children of an impoverished society and would probably be dead within a few years. (Almost half of the children born in Haiti die before the age of twelve.)

I was frozen in upset. Before I could react, the waiter saw my predicament. He quickly came back to my table and pulled down the window shade. Then he said, "Don't let them bother you, sir. Don't let them bother you. Enjoy your meal." As if it would have been possible to have enjoyed my meal after having seen those desperate children! However, don't we all do what that waiter did? Don't we all pull down the shade? Don't we all close out the hungry people of the world?

There are millions of them out there. Millions of incarnations of the resurrected Jesus, and they are suffering from malnutrition and dying from diseases that they have no strength to resist. They live without hope. They live without help. But in the face of these realities, we go on living our affluent lives. We eat our meals, drink our milk and have our desserts while, concealed from our eyes, they writhe in desperate suffering.

The church has begun to respond to the needs of the poor, but not on the scale that the Lord expects. It seems to me that the church may have forgotten its purpose and *raison d'être.* For instance, the leaders of institutionalized religion have spent over one hundred and eighty billion dollars on putting up church buildings across the country. These are buildings that are, for the most part, used for only a few hours a week on Sunday morning. I have to ask whether Jesus would rather have had that one hundred and eighty billion dollars spent on buildings or have had it used to feed the hungry children of the world. I would **103** like to know what the Lord has to say about the churches who wrap up one hundred and eighty million dollars in buildings while the children in Haiti and Ethiopia die because they don't have their basic needs met. It almost seems ludicrous to spend all of that money to honor someone who said, "I dwell not in temples made with hands."

I believe it is about time that the church gets its priorities straightened out. We who are members of the church must be reminded that the church does not exist to be served and to be the receiver of gifts. Instead, the church exists in order to serve and to give itself away to others. Just as Jesus was rich and became poor for our sake, so the rich churches of America must become poor for the sake of those who are hurting. We must learn that the best gift we can give to Jesus is to live to serve the least of our brothers and sisters and to give our wealth to meet their needs.

It should be obvious to us that the money we give to the institutional church is, for the most part, money that we give to ourselves. We buy pews and cushions so that we can sit in them. We buy stained glass windows so that we can appreciate their color. We purchase organs and buy choir robes so that we can enjoy music presented with dignity. And we pay for a minister so that we ourselves might be spiritually fed. Most of the money that we give to Christian causes ends up being used for our own benefit. People often say, "We've got to take care of ourselves or we can't take care of anybody else. We have to provide for our own needs before we can consider the needs of anyone else." There is a certain degree of truth and logic to such statements, but I want to point out that Jesus said that only those who are willing to lose their lives will find them and only those who are willing to die will live. I am absolutely convinced that Jesus' statement is not only applicable to individuals, but is also applicable to the body of Christ. Only the church that is willing to lose itself will find itself. Only the church that is willing to die will be capable of living. Only the church that gives its resources to the poor and oppressed will survive.

Søren Kierkegaard, the Danish philosopher-theologian, once described how he went into the great cathedral in Copenhagen and sat in a cushioned seat and watched as sunlight streamed through stained glass windows. He saw the pastor, dressed in a velvet robe, take his place behind the mahogany pulpit, open a gilded Bible, mark it with a silk marker and read, "Jesus said, 'If any man be my disciple he must deny himself, sell whatsoever he has, give to the poor and take up his cross and follow me.'" Kierkegaard said, "As I looked around the room I was amazed that nobody was laughing." Kierkegaard was trying to communicate to us that there is something ludicrous about a religious institution that spends its resources on itself and at the same time claims to be following Jesus, who was more concerned about the poor than He was about buildings made of stone and mortar.

One of my favorite stories is about a man who goes on a tour of an oil refinery. The tour guide shows him the various aspects of the refining process and the various departments in which those processes are carried out. At the end of the tour the man asks the guide a simple question. "Where is the shipping department?"

The guide responds, "Shipping department? What shipping department?"

The man answers, "I'm looking for the place where all the gasoline and oil products in this plant are shipped out for use in the world at large."

105

"Oh," said the tour guide, "you don't understand. All the energy generated in this refinery is used up keeping the refinery going."

Such a story is a good parable of the church, for sometimes I have the feeling that most of the wealth and energy generated by the church is used in keeping the church going instead of being used to minister to the needs of those within whom the resurrected Christ has chosen to incarnate Himself. The Bible teaches that God identifies with the poor and the oppressed, and that anybody who would love Him must love them. If you're thinking that I have made it difficult for rich people to enter into the kingdom of heaven, and for churches that spend disproportionate amounts of money on their programs and buildings to be Christian, you must remember that I am not the one who first stated, that it is harder for a rich man to enter the kingdom of heaven than for a camel to go through the eye of a needle (see Mark 10:25).

When Jesus saved us, He saved us for a high and holy purpose. He saved us in order that He might use us to meet the needs of others. He saved us in order that He might begin to transform His world into the kind of world that He willed for it to be when He created it. When He saved us, He saved us in order that we might be conduits through which His love could flow into the lives of the hurting people of the world. When Jesus saved us, He saved us to be agents of a great revolution, the end of which will come when the kingdoms of this world will become the Kingdom of our God.

When we realize the purpose of our salvation, when we grasp why it is that Jesus saved us, we will know what our purpose in life is. There will no longer be doubts about what we were meant to be or to accomplish. Through Christ there is a purpose for living.

I am not ashamed of the Gospel of Christ, because it is a Gospel through which my need for a purpose for living is clearly revealed.

CHAPTER SEVEN

Jesus Meets Our Need for Hope

I am not ashamed of the Gospel of Christ, because it is superior to the messages and teachings of all the other great world religions. Other religions have high ethical teachings, intensely dedicated followers and magnificent rituals for worship. However, only Jesus offers the world the kind of hope that can generate the spirit of optimism that is essential for joyful living. Only Christianity clearly outlines a course for human history that ends in the glorious triumph of good over evil.

Those who follow the religion of Zoroastrianism believe that history is a struggle between the forces of light and forces of darkness, but the followers of Zoroaster have no assurance as to which of the two forces will win in the end. Buddhism teaches that this world is nothing but an endless cycle of sufferings, and the followers of Buddha can only hope for the Nirvana that lies outside the sphere of history in which all consciousness is lost and personal identity is abolished. Hinduism teaches that the world in which we live is basically unreal and that sooner or later this world and all in it will return to Brahma from which it has come, leaving no trace that we ever were, and assuring us that history had no significance. Only the biblical message gives us firm assurance that the history of humanity is not a tale told by an idiot, but is a purposeful unfolding of a great plan by God which will end in His establishing His Kingdom on earth as it is in heaven.

There are many who ask how I can remain so optimistic about the future of human history in light of contemporary circumstances in the world. Among my colleagues in the field of social science there are a host of prophets of doom. There are demographers who give evidence that the exponential growth of the world's population will soon put such a strain on the resources and food available on our planet as to reduce all of human existence to the barest subsistence level, if, indeed, humanity survives at all. There are ecologists who point out that we are polluting the atmosphere at such a rate that we are destroying the ozone level that filters out the dangerous rays that cause cancer and that it is only a matter of time before massive doses of infrared and ultraviolet light will render physical survival impossible. These ecologists further warn us that we are polluting the oceans at such a rate that we are destroying the plankton necessary not only for the sustenance of certain forms of ocean life but essential for the production of the oxygen which human beings must breathe. There are political scientists whose study of the escalation of the arms race leads them to predict the certain demise of civilization through an inevitable nuclear holocaust. And there are criminologists who predict the complete breakdown of law and order in the Western world, reducing human beings to barbarism at worst and to another dark age at best.

112

In the face of all these predictions, I still affirm
the Good News that God's Kingdom will come. The
world will not be destroyed by overpopulation, eco-
logical disaster, nuclear holocaust, a breakdown of
law and order or any of the other disasters that are
so casually suggested to us through the media. We
Christians are the proclaimers of the Good News of
God in the face of all this bad news. We are the ones
who are absolutely convinced that though the whole
creation groans and is in travail even up to this present
moment, salvation will come to pass and God will
preserve His creation and gloriously perfect it to His
glory (Rom. 8:21–28). The world will not end with
a bang as some suggest, nor will it end with a whimper
as T. S. Eliot, the famed English poet, suggested.
Revelation 11:15 tells us this is the way the world
will end: "The kingdoms of this world [will become]
the kingdoms of our Lord . . . and he shall reign
for ever and ever" (KJV). Hallelujah! Hallelujah!

Oscar Cullmann, one of the most important postwar
theologians, has given an illustration that helps put
the future of history in biblical perspective. Drawing
from his experiences in World War II, Cullmann reminds us of the importance of D-Day and V-Day.
Those of us who were around in the 1940s remember
D-Day, that crucial day when the Allied Forces crossed
the English Channel and landed on the beaches of
Normandy. The Nazi army arrayed itself along the
French beachhead and tried to drive the Allied Forces
back into the sea. The Nazis knew that whichever side
was victorious on that day would eventually win the
war. The Allies were convinced that the destiny of
Europe and perhaps the world would be determined

113

by what occurred in the first twenty-four hours of that battle.

Every student of history knows that the Allies prevailed and established a beachhead from which they moved forth to reclaim Europe from Nazi domination. However, many, many months of fighting and bloodshed were to follow D-Day before the final victory over the Nazis was to become a reality. The painful struggles that followed the great victory on the beaches of Normandy would cost the lives of millions of people. There would be more bombing and devastation after D-Day than had occurred before it. However, from D-Day on, there was never any question in anybody's mind that the victory would belong to the Allies. It was for that reason that, following D-Day, General Rommel joined the plot to assassinate Hitler. He knew that the war was lost on D-Day, and it was only a matter of time before the entire Third Reich would come tumbling down.

The Allies struggled and experienced numerous setbacks, the most horrendous being the Battle of the Bulge. But they never lost sight of the fact that victory would be theirs. In their most downcast moments, they were aware that it was only a matter of time before the enemy would have to give up. The decisive battle fought on D-Day enabled them to hope with the hope that transcends wishful thinking, even in the midst of the most desperate of conditions. They always knew that V-Day would come.

Cullmann makes the point that we Christians must recognize that we too are living between a D-Day and V-Day. God's D-Day was two thousand years ago on a hill called Calvary. There the God who had invaded

114

His lost creation through His son Jesus Christ confronted the awesome powers of darkness in the most crucial battle in cosmic history. When that terrible Friday had ended, it looked as though the demonic host had triumphed and that the Prince of Glory was sealed and defeated in a borrowed tomb. But that was Friday. Three days later Jesus rolled the stone away and became *Christus Victor.* He had brought the powers of darkness to nothing.

While the decisive battle was fought and won on God's D-Day, it must be recognized that His V-Day has not yet come. His V-Day is the day when a trumpet will sound and ultimate victory will be declared. His V-Day is the day when Satan will be bound and be thrown into the lake of fire. His V-Day is the day when the Lord will return and become the acknowledged King of His creation. Jesus shall reign where'er the sun does his successive journeys run. He shall put all enemies under His feet and ultimately every knee shall bow and every tongue shall confess Him Lord of all.

God has begun to create the perfect world that He will establish at His coming. He has begun to create it in us and through us, here and now. We are people through whom He wants to carry out His revolution, and He assures us that the good work that He initiates in us will come to ultimate fruition when He returns in glory. In us He has begun a movement through which He is going to eliminate poverty, overcome racism, destroy sexism, and establish a new and just societal order. The Kingdom is already breaking out in our midst. We are the first fruits of what is to become.

115

There are those who will not believe this incredible Good News and hence become cynically laid back at this exciting juncture in the human adventure. They scoff at us and say, "Who are you kidding? The world will always be a mess. You can't change things. There is no hope for this world." To those pseudosophisticated cynics I reply, "I've been reading the Bible. I've peeked at the last chapter to see how it ends—*Jesus wins!!!!!!*"

I belong to a Black church in West Philadelphia. I've been a member of that church for decades, and for me Mt. Carmel Baptist Church is the closest thing to heaven this side of the pearly gates. I preach to a lot of congregations, but I have to say that no other group of people leaves me with excitement like the congregation of my home church. People in my congregation always let me know how I'm doing. Whether I am good or bad, they let me know what they are feeling about my message.

One time when I was preaching I sensed that nothing was happening. There seemed to be no movement of the dynamism of God. I was struggling, as you have seen ministers struggle, and seemed to be getting nowhere. I had gotten about three quarters of the way through my sermon when some lady on the back row yelled, "Help him, Jesus! Help him, Jesus!" That was all the evidence I needed that things were not going well that day.

116

On the other hand, when the preacher is really "on" in my church, they let him know. The deacons sit right under the pulpit, and whenever the preacher says something especially good, they cheer him on by yelling, "Preach, brother! Preach, brother! Preach, man, preach!" And I want to tell you that when they do that to me, it makes me want to preach!

The women in my church have a special way of responding when the preacher is "doing good." They usually wave one hand in the air and call out to the preacher, "Well, well." Whenever they do that to me, my hormones bubble.

But that's not all. When I really get going, the men in my congregation shout encouragement by saying, "Keep going, brother! Keep going! Keep going!" I assure you that a preacher never gets that kind of reaction from a white congregation. White people never yell, "Keep going! Keep going!" White audiences are more likely to check their watches and mumble, "Stop! Stop!"

One Good Friday there were seven of us preaching back to back. When it was my turn to preach, I rolled into high gear, and I want to tell you, I was good. The more I preached, the more the people in that congregation "turned on," and the more they "turned on," the better I got. I got better and better and better. I got so good that I wanted to take notes on me! At the end of my message, the congregation broke loose. I was absolutely thrilled to hear the hallelujahs and the cries of joy that broke loose throughout the place. I sat down next to my pastor and he looked at me with a smile. He reached down with his hand and squeezed my knee. "You did all right, boy!" he said. (I must admit that I hate it when he calls me "boy"!)

I turned to him and asked, "Pastor, are you going to be able to top that?"

117

IT'S FRIDAY,
BUT SUNDAY'S COMIN'

The old man smiled at me and he said, "Son, you just sit back, 'cause this old man is going to do you in!"

I didn't figure that anybody could have done me in that day. I had been so good. . . . But the old guy got up, and I have to admit, he did me in. The amazing thing was that he did it with the use of one line. For an hour and a half he preached one line over and over again. For an hour and a half he stood that crowd on its ear with just one line. That line was "It's Friday, but Sunday's comin'!" That statement may not blow you away, but you should have heard him do it. He started his sermon real softly by saying, "It was Friday; it was Friday and my Jesus was dead on the tree. But that was Friday, and Sunday's comin'!"

One of the deacons yelled, "Preach, brother! Preach!" It was all the encouragement that he needed. He came on louder as he said, "It was Friday and Mary was cryin' her eyes out. The disciples were runnin' in every direction, like sheep without a shepherd, but that was Friday, and Sunday's comin'!" People in the congregation were beginning to pick up the message. Women were waving their hands in the air and calling softly, "Well, well." Some of the men were yelling, "Keep going! Keep going!"

The preacher kept going. He picked up the volume still more and shouted, "It was Friday. The cynics were lookin' at the world and sayin', 'As things have been so they shall be. You can't change anything in this world; you can't change anything.' But those cynics didn't know that it was only Friday. Sunday's comin'!

"It was Friday! And on Friday, those forces that oppress the poor and make the poor to suffer were in control. But that was Friday! Sunday's comin'!

"It was Friday, and on Friday Pilate thought he had washed his hands of a lot of trouble. The Pharisees were struttin' around, laughin' and pokin' each other in the ribs. They thought they were back in charge of things, but they didn't know that it was only Friday! Sunday's comin'!"

He kept on working that one phrase for a half hour, then an hour, then an hour and a quarter, then an hour and a half. Over and over he came at us, "It's Friday, but Sunday's comin'! It's Friday, but Sunday's comin'! It's Friday, but Sunday's comin'!"

By the time he had come to the end of the message, I was exhausted. He had me and everybody else so worked up that I don't think any of us could have stood it much longer. At the end of his message he just yelled at the top of his lungs, "IT'S FRIDAY!" and all five hundred of us in that church yelled back with one accord, "SUNDAY'S COMIN'!"

That's the Good News. That is the word that the world is waiting to hear. That's what we have got to go out there and tell the world's people. When they are psychologically depressed, we have to tell them that Sunday's coming. When they feel that they can never know love again, we have got to tell them that Sunday's coming. When they have lost their belief in the miraculous so that they no longer expect great things from God, we must tell them that Sunday's coming.

We must go to a world that is suffering economic injustice and political oppression and tell them that

119

IT'S FRIDAY,
BUT SUNDAY'S COMIN'

Sunday's coming. The world may be filled with five million hungry. Half of the planet may be under the tyranny of communist domination. Dictators may rule in Latin America; people may find their rights abridged and their hopes under attack. But I am not ashamed of the Gospel of Christ, because to all of those who are on the brink of despair, I can yell at the top of my lungs, "IT'S FRIDAY, BUT SUNDAY'S COMIN'!"